FOCUS ON
IRISH HISTORY

Gerard Brockie
Raymond Walsh

Gill & Macmillan

Published in Ireland by
Gill & Macmillan Ltd
Goldenbridge
Dublin 8

with associated companies throughout the world

© Gerard Brockie and Raymond Walsh 1993
© Artwork, Gill & Macmillan 1993

0 7171 2083 X

Print origination in Ireland by Seton Music Graphics Ltd, Bantry, Co. Cork
Colour reproduction by Kulor Centre, Dublin

Acknowledgements

For permission to reproduce colour transparencies and photographs, grateful acknowledgement is made
to the following:

Office of Public Works, Dublin; Zefa; Department of the Environment for Northern Ireland – Historic
Monuments and Buildings Branch; National Museum of Ireland; British Library; Michael Holford;
National Gallery of Ireland; Bord Fáilte; E.T. Archive; Ulster Museum; Atlas van Stolk, Rotterdam;
National Army Museum, London; A.F. Kersting; Trinity College, Dublin; National Portrait Gallery,
London; Michael Scully; Scala; Derry Museum; Bank of Ireland.
   The reconstruction of Glendalough is by Stephen Conlin and is reproduced with his kind permission.
The reconstructions of Dundrum Castle, Grey Abbey and a Norman Motte are reproduced with the kind
permission of the Department of the Environment for Northern Ireland – Historic Monuments and
Buildings Branch.

Other illustrations: Joanne Hugo
Original design and maps: Design Works
Additional maps: Unlimited Design

Contents

IRELAND IN 1100

IRELAND AROUND 1100

Life in Ireland around 1100 would seem very strange to us today. Instead of towns and cities most people lived in the countryside, where they depended on agriculture for their livelihood. Cattle were highly valued and people often went to war in order to carry off their neighbours' livestock.

Nowadays the country is divided into two States, the Republic of Ireland and Northern Ireland. However, around 1100 there were several small kingdoms in the land, each ruled by its own king. These kingdoms or *tuaths* frequently went to war against one another.

The Irish language (Gaelic) was used throughout the country at the time. Even the Vikings who had arrived here from about 800 onwards had learnt Irish in order to trade with the local population.

Compared with the large towns and cities in modern Ireland the few towns which existed 900 years ago were very small indeed. As the Gaelic Irish lived in the countryside, towns such as Dublin, Cork, Limerick and Waterford had been founded by the Vikings. They were small, with narrow streets and full of dirt and disease. Each town had walls surrounding it as a protection against attack from Gaelic kings.

Despite all the warfare at the time, Ireland was a land which possessed many monasteries and churches. Even the most warlike kings founded new monasteries, often as burial places for themselves and their

Glendalough, Co. Wicklow, one of the most important monasteries in Ireland around 1100.

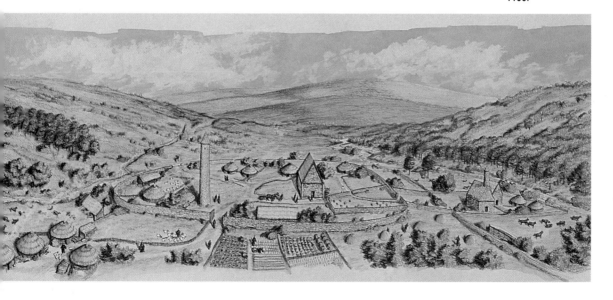

families. As well as assisting the sick, the poor and travellers in an age before the arrival of hospitals, social welfare or hotels, the monasteries were also places to which people fled during warfare.

In order to understand how the country was ruled we must first take a look at the lives of the kings and their tuaths or communities.

KINGS AND TUATHS

The Irish were a Celtic people and in some important ways they continued the customs which the Celts had brought with them to Ireland around 500 BC. One very strong feature of Celtic societies was the tribe or extended family group. Each tribe or tuath was ruled over by a king. The king was elected by the freemen of the tuath under a system known as the *deirbhfhine*. This means that the sons, grandsons and greatgrandsons of former kings were eligible for election as king. This system led to frequent disputes over succession of the kingship, and tuaths were often divided between two or more men claiming the right to be king. In England and in many European countries, on the other hand, the king's eldest son succeeded him on the throne.

If strong foreign invaders came to Ireland the Gaelic tuaths would be in a weak position to resist because they quarrelled with each other and even within each tuath because of the elected form of kingship. This was exactly what happened when the Normans invaded Ireland from England and Wales from 1169 onwards.

While some of the Gaelic kings ruled over very small areas, others had control of large provinces such as Leinster. Many of them traced their ancestors back over a thousand years and they were very proud of this. We can still see the sites of the palaces of the more powerful kings at places like Tara in Co. Meath and Navan Fort in Co. Armagh.

Tara, Co. Meath.

Navan Fort, Co. Armagh.

TEST YOUR KNOWLEDGE
1 How did most Irish people earn their living around 1100?
2 What was a tuath?
3 Name the language spoken throughout Ireland in 1100.
4 Who founded the first Irish towns?
5 List some of the functions carried out in the monasteries.
6 How were kings chosen in Gaelic Ireland?
7 Identify two weaknesses which left the Gaelic tribes open to outside attack.

THE PEOPLE OF THE TUATH

The people of the tuath were divided into rich and poor. Next to the king came the nobles and the learned classes such as the poets, priests and judges. The judges or *Brehons* had their own type of Irish law called the *Brehon laws* – from the Irish word *breitheamh* meaning a judge. The Brehon laws are an important source for historians investigating life in Ireland around a thousand years ago.

Next in importance to the learned classes came the *freemen*. These were farmers and craftsmen who owned their own land.

The rest of the people were *unfree* members of the tuath. They were little better than slaves and could not own property or carry weapons. Many of them were people who had been captured in war.

Some of the customs of the Gaelic Irish did not accord with the rules of the Christian Church. Many kings had more than one wife, divorce was allowed in certain cases and some monks and abbots of monasteries fathered children. Indeed, the control of important monasteries like that of Armagh passed from father to son for several generations.

However, around 1100 there was a strong movement to reform the Christian Church throughout Europe. This in turn reached Ireland under the leadership of St Malachy of Armagh.

3

THE REFORM OF THE CHURCH

Between 600 and 900 Ireland had been known as the island of saints and scholars. At this time, when much of continental Europe had become pagan, scholars flocked to the Irish monasteries which became centres of holiness and learning. We can still see the magnificent craftwork of the early Irish monks in works of art like the Book of Kells and the Ardagh Chalice.

A page from the Book of Kells.

The Ardagh Chalice.

At the same time Irish monks travelled to England, Scotland and the continent of Europe where they founded monasteries and towns. As well as spreading the Christian gospel they also frequently re-introduced reading and writing to areas which had lost these arts of civilisation.

However, from around 800 onwards Viking attacks destroyed many Irish monasteries and weakened others. At the same time many of the monks had begun to lead worldly lives. Frequently the abbots of the richer monasteries were relations of the local king. Such men spent more time going to war than attending to their religious duties. Eventually matters became so bad that monks from one monastery would attack and destroy other monasteries as part of the local warfare between the various kings.

Between 1100 and 1150 some important steps were taken to reform the Church in Ireland. The leading figure in this was the archbishop of Armagh, St Malachy.

4

- Ireland was divided into dioceses under the rule of bishops with four archdioceses under archbishops at Armagh, Dublin, Tuam and Cashel. This lessened the power of the monasteries.
- Corrupt abbots of monasteries were replaced by men leading holy lives.
- Strict religious orders from Europe were introduced into Ireland. St Malachy started this movement when he brought the Cistercian Order to Mellifont, Co. Louth in 1141.

Despite the improvements brought about by St Malachy and others there were still many abuses which continued. The changes did not alter the lifestyles of the kings and their followers. Indeed, as we shall see in the next chapter, English kings and churchmen complained to the pope that the Irish were half savage and that only conquest by a foreign power would bring them into line with the rest of Europe.

TEST YOUR KNOWLEDGE
1 What were the Brehon laws?
2 List some disadvantages of the unfree members of the tuath.
3 In what way did the lifestyle in Gaelic Ireland conflict with the rules of the Christian Church?
4 Why had Ireland been known as the island of saints and scholars between 600 and 900?
5 Name the foreign invaders who attacked Irish monasteries from around 800 onwards.
6 Who led the reform of the Church in Ireland in the twelfth century?
7 Was this reform a complete success? Explain your answer.

The main monasteries founded by Irish monks abroad.

The ruins of Mellifont Abbey founded by the Cistercian Order, which was brought to Ireland by St Malachy.

KINGS AND HIGH KINGS

At the time that St Malachy and others were reforming the Church in Ireland, kings and their followers continued to go to war almost every year. As well as carrying off booty and forcing their enemies to pay tribute, some of the more powerful kings fought for the right to be recognised as high king of all Ireland. Ever since the death of King Brian Boru at the Battle of Clontarf in 1014 no single king had been strong enough to force all the other rulers to accept him as high king. Until around 1100 Brian's descendants, the O'Briens of Munster, were the most powerful rulers in Ireland. However, soon after becoming king of Connaught in 1106, Turlough O'Connor made himself the most powerful ruler in the country. In 1156 he was succeeded by his son, Rory, who was destined to be the last high king of Ireland.

By 1166 Rory O'Connor had more power than any high king since the time of Brian Boru. It appeared that people throughout Ireland were about to recognise a single overlord, the high king. This was not to be, however. In August 1166 Dermot MacMurrough, the king of Leinster, took an action that was to have momentous consequences for all of Ireland. MacMurrough, an enemy of O'Connor, had been defeated in war and expelled from his territory. Determined to gain revenge and to recover his kingdom he set sail from Ireland in search of foreign allies. His search brought him to the court of Henry II (1154-89), the Norman king of England.

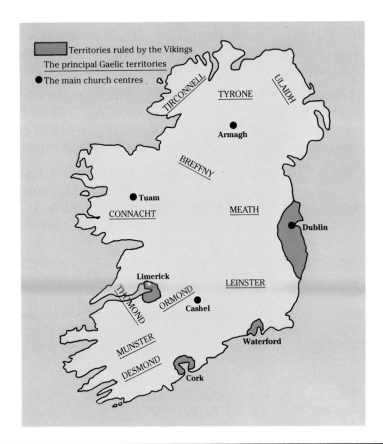

Legend on map:
- Territories ruled by the Vikings
- The principal Gaelic territories
- ● The main church centres

TIRCONNELL

TYRONE

ULAIDH

● Armagh

BREFFNY

● Tuam

CONNACHT

MEATH

● Dublin

Limerick

THOMOND

ORMOND

● Cashel

LEINSTER

MUNSTER

DESMOND

Cork

Waterford

Ireland before
the Norman
invasion.

Chapter 1: Review

- Around 1100 most people in Ireland lived in the countryside and depended on livestock and crops for their livelihood.

- At that time there were several small kingdoms or tuaths in Ireland, each ruled by its own king.

- The few towns which existed had been founded by the Vikings as centres of trade; they were small with narrow streets and were surrounded by walls as a means of defence.

- The Gaelic Irish were a Celtic people who had strong ties of kinship. Their kings were elected by a system known as deirbhfhine.

- Kings and their followers were constantly at war with other kings and peoples.

- The people of the tuath were divided into rich and poor. Next to the king came the nobles and members of the learned classes such as judges, poets or priests.

- The freemen were next in importance to the learned classes. The rest of the tuath consisted of unfree members who were little better than slaves.

- At the time many kings had more than one wife, divorce was allowed in certain circumstances and priests, bishops and abbots were often the fathers of children.

- From around 1100 onwards there was a movement to reform the Christian Church. The greatest leader of this movement was St Malachy of Armagh.

- Between 600 and 900 Ireland had been known as the island of saints and scholars. However, after the Viking invasions many of the monasteries had become corrupt, with abbots and monks leading bad lives.

- Between 1100 and 1150 there were important reforms in the Church:

dioceses were set up under the rule of bishops; corrupt abbots were replaced holy men and strict religious orders we introduced from the continent of Euro

- Powerful kings fought each other for t right to be recognised as high king. By 1166 Rory O'Connor of Connaught ha almost achieved this aim.

- In August 1166 the defeated king of Leinster, Dermot MacMurrough, left Ireland to seek help from the Norman ruler of England, King Henry II (1154-89).

ACTIVITIES

1 Complete the following sentences:
   (a) From around 800 onwards Viking attacks destroyed _____.
   (b) Around 1100 Ireland was divided into several _____.
   (c) The learned classes in Gaelic Ireland included _____.
   (d) Some of the more powerful kings fought for the right to be recognised as _____.
   (e) In August 1166 the defeated king of Leinster left Ireland to seek foreign allies. His name was _____.

2 True or false?
   (a) The Vikings refused to learn the Irish language.
   (b) When a Gaelic king died his eldest son then became king.
   (c) The Brehon laws were the system of laws in Gaelic Ireland.
   (d) Divorce was allowed in certain cases in Ireland at the time.
   (e) St Malachy was completely successful in reforming the Church in Ireland.

3 Write a short paragraph on each of the following:
   (a) Kings and warfare in Ireland around 1100.
   (b) The reform of the Church in Ireland 1100-50.

THE NORMANS ARRIVE IN IRELAND

THE NORMANS

The king of England in 1166 was Henry II (1154-89) a member of the Norman race. At this time the Normans were famous as the bravest fighters in Europe. They were a strong and powerful people who had conquered many lands. They were descendants of Vikings who had settled in Normandy in northern France. Wherever they went they brought their knowledge of warfare with them.

King Henry II (1154-89).

They built castles, monasteries and cathedrals and lived according to the feudal system. Under this system knights fought for their lords in return for a grant of land.

Southern Italy and the Holy Land were among the lands conquered by the Norman knights. Their most famous conquest, however, took place in 1066 when the Norman leader, William the Conqueror, defeated the English at the Battle of Hastings and made himself king of England.

Two scenes from the Bayeux Tapestry telling the story of the Norman conquest of England. The tapestry contains a series of pictures sewn with coloured wool on linen cloth. At (A) we can see a picture of King William's ship arriving in England and at (B) Norman cavalry attacking English footsoldiers.

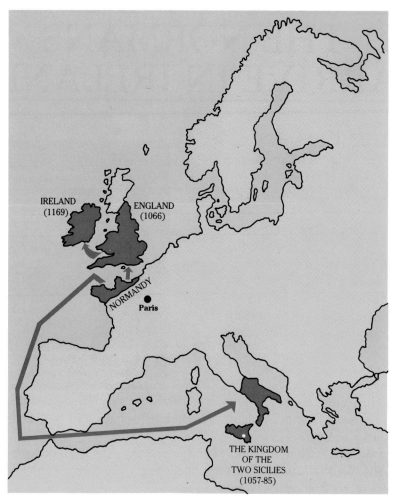

The Norman expansion in Europe in the twelfth century.

Like the soldiers of the Irish kings, the English troops at Hastings were mostly foot soldiers wielding axes. These were no match for the Norman knights on horseback and the highly skilled archers with their bows and arrows.

From the time of the Norman conquest of England in 1066 various kings considered extending their rule to Ireland. They were encouraged to do so by bishops, priests and monks who wanted to gain control over the Church in Ireland and to reform the customs of the Gaelic Irish.

Soon after becoming king of England, Henry II applied to the pope for a blessing on his plans to invade Ireland. Adrian IV, the only English-born pope ever, responded with a letter, called *Laudabiliter*, in which he named Henry II lord of Ireland. Warfare in his vast lands of France kept Henry occupied and he could not afford to consider invading Ireland during the early years of his reign. When Dermot MacMurrough arrived at his court in 1166, however, Henry regarded it as an opportunity to carry out his long-held ambition to extend Norman power to Ireland.

10

DERMOT MACMURROUGH'S BARGAIN

When Dermot met King Henry in France he recognised Henry as his overlord and received permission to go to England and recruit Norman knights for an invasion of Ireland. Dermot travelled to Bristol, where he met Richard de Clare who was also known as *Strongbow*, one of the most powerful Norman lords in England. A bargain was struck between the two. If Strongbow agreed to land in Ireland with a force of Normans, Dermot promised him his daughter, Aoife, in marriage and the right to succeed him as king of Leinster after his death. Now as this was completely against the Gaelic law of succession, Strongbow could only become ruler of Leinster if he conquered it by force of arms.

Dermot also made an agreement with two other knights, Robert Fitzstephen and Maurice Fitzgerald: they were promised the town of Wexford if they agreed to come to Ireland with their bands of soldiers. Having reached agreements with his new allies Dermot returned to Ireland to await their arrival, which was expected in the summer of 1169.

TEST YOUR KNOWLEDGE
1 *How did the Normans get their name?*
2 *What was the feudal system?*
3 *Name the most famous conquest carried out by the Normans.*
4 *Why were Norman soldiers so successful in battle?*
5 *How did Henry II show that he was interested in invading Ireland?*
6 *What agreement did Dermot MacMurrough reach with Richard de Clare (Strongbow)?*

THE ARRIVAL OF THE NORMANS

On 1 May 1169 three shiploads of Norman soldiers landed at Bannow Bay in Co. Wexford. They were led by Robert Fitzstephen and Maurice Prendergast. MacMurrough marched to meet them and together they captured the town of Wexford from its Viking rulers.

In August 1170 Strongbow himself landed near Waterford with over a thousand followers. Together with MacMurrough they captured the town of Waterford from the Vikings. The marriage of Strongbow and Aoife MacMurrough then took place in the cathedral of Waterford.

The Normans next set their sights on Dublin. The high king, Rory O'Connor, gathered a large army to the west of the town in order to defend it. MacMurrough, however, led his Gaelic and Norman forces through the Wicklow hills and surprised O'Connor by arriving outside the walls of Dublin. The Viking rulers of Dublin sent the archbishop, St Laurence O'Toole, to negotiate a peace treaty with Dermot and his followers. While these talks were going on the Normans suddenly attacked the town and took it by storm.

The marriage of Strongbow and Aoife, the daughter of Dermot MacMurrough.

Having captured Dublin, they resisted all attacks aimed at removing them. The former Viking inhabitants were expelled and the new rulers founded a castle to defend the town. This was the origin of *Dublin Castle* which was to become the centre of English government in Ireland for almost eight centuries.

When Dermot MacMurrough died suddenly in May 1171 Strongbow, according to the agreement, succeeded him as king of Leinster. He faced two major problems, however. The Gaelic Irish would never willingly accept him as king of Leinster and his own overlord, King Henry II, was concerned that Strongbow was becoming too powerful. The last thing Henry wanted to see was an independent Norman kingdom set up in Ireland. To prevent this happening and to assert his control over Ireland he decided to visit the country and see conditions for himself.

TEST YOUR KNOWLEDGE
1   *Where and when did the Normans first land in Ireland?*
2   *What was the first town in Ireland captured by the Normans?*
3   *When did Strongbow arrive in Ireland?*
4   *Where did his marriage to Aoife MacMurrough take place?*
5   *In what way did the Normans capture Dublin?*
6   *Why did Henry II decide to visit Ireland?*

Christchurch
Cathedral, Dublin,
built by the
Normans on the
site of an earlier
Viking church.

HENRY II IN IRELAND

On 17 October 1171 Henry II landed near Waterford with 500 knights and 4,000 archers. He believed rightly that with such a huge army he would not need to fight; the Irish kings would submit to him without a struggle. Henry granted Strongbow the province of Leinster as a fief in return for the service of one hundred knights. However, he kept for himself the control of the towns of Waterford, Wexford and Dublin. Leaving Waterford he set out on a slow march for Dublin, receiving the submission of many Gaelic rulers on the way.

The king reached Dublin on 11 November and remained there throughout the winter. He declared it a royal city and granted it its first charter which set out the rights and privileges of the citizens.

As the king could not remain for long in his new kingdom he had to arrange how Ireland would be governed in his absence. He decided to appoint a chief governor known as the *lord deputy* and a council of advisers to carry out this task. We shall learn more about these in chapter 4. As his first lord deputy in Ireland King Henry appointed Hugh de Lacy, a Norman lord from the Welsh borders.

While Henry was in Dublin a council of the Irish bishops met at Cashel. Realising that the pope approved of the Norman invasion, they swore an oath of loyalty to Henry II and accepted him as the lawful ruler of Ireland.

Having received the submission of the bishops and most of the Gaelic kings, and having appointed his loyal follower Hugh de Lacy to rule in his absence, Henry returned to England in April 1172 well pleased with his visit to Ireland.

Cashel, Co.
Tipperary where
the Irish bishops
met and agreed
to accept Henry II
as their overlord.

THE CONQUEST CONTINUES

When Henry returned to England the Normans continued to attack the Gaelic kings and conquer new lands for themselves and their followers. Hugh de Lacy drove the Gaelic rulers out of Meath and set up a huge province for himself there.

We have two main types of source on the activities of these Norman conquerors: the physical remains of the buildings they set up and written accounts dating from the time. The first conquerors built wooden castles for protection on man-made hills known as *mottes*. As soon as possible these were replaced by strong stone castles and walls. Look carefully at the picture of Trim Castle, the headquarters of de Lacy's kingdom of Meath. It is the largest Norman castle remaining in Ireland, and we can see for ourselves the great efforts of the Normans to protect their conquests and overawe the Gaelic people in the surrounding countryside.

The ruins of Trim Castle, Co. Meath.

Written sources for the activities of the Norman conquerors come down to us from both the Irish and Norman sides. The annals or historical accounts written in Irish monasteries were often hostile to the new arrivals. The Normans had their supporters as well, however. The two most important were a pro-French poem called *The Song of Dermot and the Earl* and the writings of Gerald of Wales, a priest who was related to many of the leading Norman conquerors.

For example, *The Song of Dermot and the Earl* contained a reference to de Lacy's activities at Trim:

> Then Hugh de Lacy
> Fortified a house at Trim
> And threw a trench around it,
> And then enclosed it with a stockade

Gerald of Wales wrote a whole book called *The Conquest of Ireland*, in which he always defended the action of the Normans and looked down on the Gaelic Irish as a barbarous people.

While de Lacy was capturing Meath other Normans were attacking parts of Leinster and Munster. In 1174 Strongbow's attack on Munster received a setback when he was defeated by Rory O'Connor and Donal O'Brien at the Battle of Thurles. After the high king and his followers followed this up with a victory over the Normans in Meath there was an attempt to reach an agreement between the Normans and the Gaelic Irish.

After prolonged discussions Henry II and Rory O'Connor reached an agreement known as the *Treaty of Windsor* in 1175. Ireland was divided into two sections, one Irish and the other Norman. O'Connor recognised Henry as his overlord and agreed to collect taxes for the English king from other Gaelic rulers. However, he had no authority over the Normans in Ireland who were directly subject to Henry.

While O'Connor tried to carry out the terms of the Treaty of Windsor Henry II soon broke it by allowing Norman lords to conquer more land in Ireland. In the next chapter we shall examine one of the most spectacular of these efforts: the conquest of Ulster by the Norman adventurer, John de Courcy.

Windsor Castle where a treaty between Henry II and Rory O'Connor was agreed in 1175.

TEST YOUR KNOWLEDGE
1 When did Henry II arrive in Ireland?
2 What grant did he make to Strongbow?
3 Name the towns which he kept under his own control.
*4 Describe the arrangements which Henry made for the government of
    Ireland in his absence.*
5 What occurred at the meeting of the Irish bishops at Cashel?
6 Who was Hugh de Lacy?
7 Where were his new lands situated?
8 Name one written source for the Norman conquest of Ireland.

Chapter 2: Review

- The king of England in 1166, Henry II (1154-89), was a member of the Norman race. These were famous as conquerors and were descended from Vikings who came to live in the French area of Normandy.

- In 1066 the Normans gained control of England after the victory of their leader, William the Conqueror, at the Battle of Hastings.

- From then onwards a number of English kings considered invading Ireland, including Henry II who got permission from the pope to do so.

- When Dermot MacMurrough met Henry II in France he agreed to accept Henry as his overlord. In turn Henry gave him permission to recruit Norman knights in England for an invasion of Ireland.

- In England Dermot reached agreement with a number of Norman lords, including Richard de Clare (Strongbow). He promised Strongbow his daughter's hand in marriage and his own kingdom of Leinster after his death.

- In May 1169 three shiploads of Normans landed at Bannow Bay in Wexford. MacMurrough came to meet them and together they captured the town of Wexford from its Viking rulers.

- In August 1170 Strongbow landed near Waterford with over a thousand soldiers. He joined MacMurrough's forces, captured Waterford and married Dermot's daughter, Aoife, in Waterford Cathedral.

- In September 1170 the Normans avoided the force of the high king, Rory O'Connor, and succeeded in capturing the city of Dublin.

- On the death of MacMurrough in May 1171 Strongbow succeeded him. However, Henry II, fearful that the Normans were becoming too powerful, decided to go to Ireland and assert his control over them.

- While in Ireland Henry II received the submission of the Irish kings and of the bishops and appointed Hugh de Lacy as lord deputy to rule the country in his absence.

- After Henry's return to England, the Normans pressed ahead with the conquest of Ireland. In 1175 an agreement known as the Treaty of Windsor was signed between Rory O'Connor and Henry II, dividing Ireland into Norman and Gaelic areas.

- While O'Connor tried to carry out the terms of the Treaty of Windsor, Henry II soon broke it and allowed his Norman followers to conquer more territories in Ireland.

ACTIVITIES

Multiple choice

(a) Strongbow was the other name given to: (i) Maurice Prendergast; (ii) Richard de Clare; (iii) John de Courcy; (iv) Robert Fitzstephen.

(b) In 1175 Rory O'Connor and Henry II reached an agreement known as the Treaty of: (i) Mellifont; (ii) London; (iii) Waterford; (iv) Windsor.

(c) The Norman conquest of England took place in: (i) 1066; (ii) 1106; (iii) 1166; (iv) 1056.

(d) The first lord deputy appointed by Henry II to rule Ireland was: (i) Strongbow; (ii) John de Courcy; (iii) Hugh de Lacy; (iv) Dermot MacMurrough.

Match an item in column 1 with a item in column 2

COLUMN 1	COLUMN 2
A High King	Laurence O'Toole
An ally to Dermot MacMurrough	William the Conqueror
A Lord Deputy	Strongbow
Archbishop of Dublin	Hugh de Lacy
A king of England	Rory O'Connor

Draw up a time chart of the main events in the Norman conquest of Ireland between 1166 and 1175.

Write a paragraph on the role of Dermot MacMurrough in the Norman conquest.

CHAPTER 3

JOHN DE COURCY AND THE NORMAN CONQUEST OF ULSTER

THE NORMANS ARRIVE IN ULSTER

The arrival of the Normans in Ulster followed a pattern similar to the story of Dermot MacMurrough in Leinster. At the time Ulster was divided into a number of Gaelic kingdoms stretching from the Cenel Connaill in Donegal to the McDunlevy lands in Down. It was the leader of the McDunlevy kingdom of Ulaid (Antrim and Down) who invited the Normans under John de Courcy to assist him in his wars against other Gaelic tribes.

De Courcy was a young knight from Somerset in England who had come to Ireland in search of land and adventure. Early in 1177 he set out from Dublin with an army of 300 followers marching behind his family flag, the eagle standard. De Courcy intended not merely to assist McDunlevy but instead to conquer his lands. A number of hard-fought battles took place in Down and Antrim, but de Courcy's army emerged victorious due to its combination of knights on horseback and skilled Norman archers. His victories in battle ensured that he replaced

John de Courcy.

McDunlevy as ruler of Ulaid, giving himself the title prince of Ulster. We can read about de Courcy's adventures in an heroic poem written at the time and recorded in the *Book of Howth*. Although this poem is biased in favour of de Courcy it gives us much interesting information concerning his exploits.

In 1180 in order to forge a useful military alliance de Courcy married Africa, the daughter of King Godred of the Isle of Man. Having conquered his province of Ulaid de Courcy then set about defending it with a network of towns and castles.

CARRICKFERGUS CASTLE

The new ruler of eastern Ulster chose Carrickfergus as his head-quarters and the site of his strongest castle. Even today visitors to Carrickfergus marvel at the high towers and strong walls designed by the Norman rulers. It was one of the earliest stone castles begun by the Normans in Ireland, and, together with Trim Castle in Co. Meath, provides us with valuable information on the defence plans and general lifestyle of the Norman conquerors.

Begun under de Courcy as early as 1178, work continued on Carrick-fergus Castle until around 1250. It was always the most important castle in Ulster and, according to a government record of the time, its garrison in 1212 consisted of forty men, twice the size of any other castle garrison in Ulster.

A reconstruction of
Carrickfergus Castle
as it appeared in
Norman times.

19

When at Carrickfergus Castle de Courcy lived like a lord. At least 200 people were in attendance when he resided there. He carried out his public duties in the great hall. These would have included hearing court cases, discussing matters of government and greeting important visitors such as bishops, Irish kings or English lords.

On the third floor of the castle were the earl's private quarters. As earl of Ulster, de Courcy enjoyed spacious rooms with fine windows overlooking the sea. His followers had to be content with the smaller rooms on the floor beneath, where they acted as a protection against any attack on their master.

The Norman castle at Dundrum, Co. Down, now and then.

As well as Carrickfergus Castle there are other splendid remains at Dundrum and Greencastle, Co. Down, to remind us of the life and times of de Courcy and his successors, the earls of Ulster. Not only did they introduce castle building into Ulster, they also brought something which has proved far more enduring: the building of towns.

TOWNS AND TOWNSPEOPLE

We have seen already that the Gaelic Irish lived mostly in the countryside and that large-scale settlements of people were generally not a feature of Gaelic society. The only exceptions grew up around monastic sites such as Armagh and Downpatrick. However, these were not towns in the true sense because their inhabitants did not earn their living from crafts and trade or enjoy a high degree of self-government.

Despite the fact that Ulster was probably the poorest area in Ireland at the time, and that attack from Gaelic rulers was a constant threat, the Normans succeeded in establishing a number of thriving towns in the earldom of Ulster. Apart from Carrickfergus these included Coleraine, Downpatrick, Newtownards and Antrim. Others, such as Carnmoney, Belfast and Portrush, although towns in name were really only villages. Some towns were started anew whereas others were developed on the site of existing monastic settlements. De Courcy and his successors succeeded in attracting settlers from England with names such as Logan, Russell, Savage and Hackett. These names are still found in Down and Antrim to this day.

Although a number of towns were thriving centres of activity, such as Coleraine where a bridge was built across the River Bann in 1248, Carrickfergus stood head and shoulders above the rest in terms of size and importance.

We are fortunate regarding the principal town in medieval Ulster because its central street plan has remained unchanged ever since. In addition to this there have been a number of extensive archaeological excavations at Carrickfergus which have shed a good deal of light on the story of the town. Both craftsmen and traders lived side by side. The remains of a pottery kiln dating from around 1200 were unearthed in High Street. We also know from archaeology that the people of Carrickfergus traded mainly with Scotland and north-west England, though they also ventured further afield. A Carrickfergus-registered boat was wrecked off the coast of France in 1308 carrying a cargo of wine from Gascony. It has been estimated that the population of the town around this time was almost a thousand people.

llery and
ry found
ıg
vations at
ckfergus.

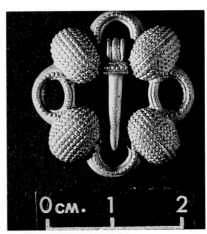 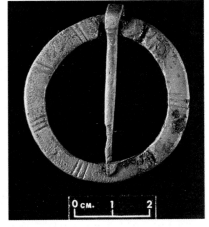

Crafts and trade were carried on in addition to the town's role as the centre of English government in Ulster. A further source of wealth for Carrickfergus was as a market town where the produce of the local countryside was brought and sold.

TEST YOUR KNOWLEDGE

1 Where was the Gaelic kingdom of Ulaid?
2 Explain why de Courcy and his followers were successful in battle.
3 What was recorded in the Book of Howth?
4 Where was the headquarters of the earl of Ulster?
5 Name three towns established by the Normans in Ulster.
6 List one important archaeological find made at Carrickfergus.

The earldom of
Ulster at its great
extent around 13

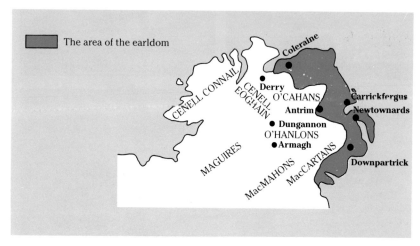

The area of the earldom

FARMING THE LAND

As in the rest of Ireland, the Normans in Ulster hoped to become wealthy from the ownership of land. Indeed, the Norman invasions of different countries were part of an overall trend based on land hunger in Europe at the time. The population was increasing rapidly and there were only two ways to acquire more land: by reclaiming poor land from bogs or mountains, or by armed conquest.

The Normans in Ireland hoped to grow large amounts of grain for the English market. To do this they would first have to establish an English-type economy based on the manor with underlords to rent large farms and peasants to work the land.

Although they succeeded in introducing this system for a while into southern areas like Kilkenny and Tipperary, they were far less successful in Ulster. Because only parts of Down and Antrim were under English control, farmers were under constant threat of attack from the Gaelic Irish. A sufficient number of English settlers could never be encouraged to come to Ireland, and Norman settlers had to allow large numbers of Irish tenants or *betaghs* on to their lands.

From around 1300 onwards the population declined rapidly, as we shall see in chapter 5. This reduced the need for corn-growing, and more and more land was turned over to cattle and sheep-rearing in Ulster and throughout Ireland.

At around the same time unfree tenants such as serfs and betaghs were able to achieve better conditions since workers were in demand owing to the falling population. As in England, they were able to replace their duty to work on the lord's land with a money rent instead.

CHURCH AND MONASTERIES

As in Europe and England, the Normans were to become great patrons of the Church in Ireland. Indeed, one of the first actions of Henry II had been to secure the support of the pope and the Irish bishops. In return he guaranteed the privileges and wealth of the Church. At a time when few besides churchmen could read and write, kings and lords used the talents of bishops and priests to help govern the country. The Normans in Ireland continued this trend. The advice of bishops, monks and priests was frequently sought by rulers like de Courcy and there were usually a number of bishops on the king's council which advised his representative in Ireland, the lord deputy.

The remains of Inch Abbey which was founded by John de Courcy.

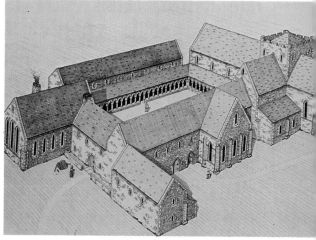

Grey Abbey, Co. Down, now and then.

The activities of John de Courcy regarding the Church in Ulster were typical of great Norman lords elsewhere in Ireland. He founded Cistercian abbeys at Inch and Grey in Co. Down and invited monks from the north of England to run them. Downpatrick Cathedral was reconstructed and Benedictine monks were introduced from England to provide the services.

In Carrickfergus itself the parish church of St Nicholas was reconstructed on a large scale. It was the Normans who introduced regular parishes into Ireland. Each parish was in the care of its parish priest, and people were bound to pay one tenth of their income (*tithes*) to the upkeep of the parish.

St Nicholas's Church, Carrickfergus.

Because the Cathedral of Connor lay outside the control of the earl of Ulster, St Nicholas's church in Carrickfergus was frequently used as a substitute or pro-cathedral instead. The bishop often stayed at Carrickfergus to advise the earl and his officials. The western part of Co. Down not under Norman rule was converted into a separate diocese, the diocese of Dromore, under the control of the Gaelic Irish.

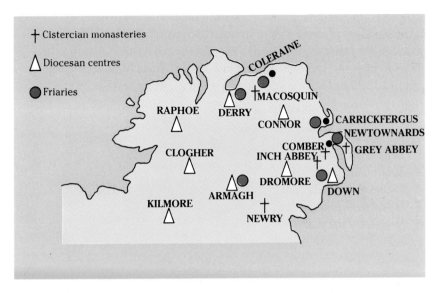

- ✝ Cistercian monasteries
- △ Diocesan centres
- ⬤ Friaries

COLERAINE

✝MACOSQUIN

RAPHOE DERRY CONNOR CARRICKFERGUS

NEWTOWNARDS

CLOGHER COMBER GREY ABBEY
INCH ABBEY

ARMAGH DROMORE DOWN

KILMORE NEWRY

...urch in
...al Ulster.

From the 1220s a new type of religious order arrived in Ireland from Europe: the mendicant or begging friars. Unlike the monks who lived in monasteries in the countryside, the friars lived in small friaries in the towns. The two largest orders, the Franciscans and the Dominicans, in particular established houses in many Norman towns in Ireland.

Six friaries were founded in Ulster in the thirteenth century, namely at Armagh, Carrickfergus, Coleraine, Derry, Downpatrick and Newtownards. The remains of these churches may still be seen at Armagh and Newtownards.

At the same time as these developments were taking place in the earldom the Church in the rest of Ulster remained under the control of Gaelic bishops and abbots, who frequently continued the customs which had been condemned by St Malachy and other reformers.

The ruins of the medieval priory at Newtownards.

The changing fortunes of both the Gaelic rulers of Ulster and the Norman lords of the earldom frequently mirrored wider developments throughout Ireland. In the next two chapters we shall examine these and see how the Norman colony enjoyed a period of prosperity up to around 1300 only to be followed by a era of decay and decline.

TEST YOUR KNOWLEDGE

1 *Explain the existence of land hunger in Europe around 1100.*
2 *Why were English settlers reluctant to come to Ireland?*
3 *What was the attitude of Henry II to the Church in Ireland?*
4 *Name two monasteries founded by John de Courcy.*
5 *What were tithes?*
6 *Who were the friars?*

THE EARLS OF ULSTER

John de Courcy	1177-1205
Hugh de Lacy	1205-1243*
Walter de Burgo	1264-1271
Richard de Burgo, The 'Red Earl'	1271-1326
William de Burgo, The 'Brown Earl'	1326-1333

* Between 1243 and 1254 King Henry III of England held the Earldom of Ulster. From 1254 to 1264 it was held by his eldest son, Prince Edward, who was also lord of Ireland at the time.

Chapter 3: Review

- In 1177 a Norman adventurer, John de Courcy, and his band of followers carried out a successful attack on the McDunlevy kingdom of Ulaid (Antrim and Down).

- De Courcy took the title earl of Ulster and set up his headquarters at Carrickfergus where he had a castle built.

- Carrickfergus Castle was one of the earliest stone castles constructed by the Normans in Ireland. Here de Courcy, and his successors as earls, lived in splendid apartments and carried out the government of the earldom.

- As well as at Carrickfergus the Normans constructed several other castles in Ulster, including those at Dundrum and Greencastle in Co. Down where extensive remains may still be seen.

- The Normans introduced towns to Ulster which became thriving centres trade and craftwork. Apart from Carrickfergus these included Coleraine Downpatrick, Newtownards, Antrim and Carnmoney.

- Carrickfergus was by far the largest town in Norman times. The discoveries of archaeologists have given us much

...formation about the lives of its medieval inhabitants.

...s in the rest of Ireland, the Normans introduced new methods of farming to Ulster based on the system of the manor. However, they were always at a disadvantage because of the shortage of English settlers in the area.

...rom around 1300 the population decreased rapidly. This reduced the need for corn-growing, and more and more land was turned over to the rearing of cattle and sheep.

...s in Europe and England, the Normans were generous patrons of the Church in Ireland. They founded many churches and monasteries.

- Bishops, priests and monks were often part of the government of kings and lords and a number of bishops usually sat on the council that advised the king's lord deputy in Ireland.

- In his earldom of Ulster John de Courcy founded many churches, including the Cistercian abbeys at Inch and Grey in Co. Down.

- From the 1220s a new type of religious order arrived in Ireland: the friars. By 1300 there were six friaries founded in Ulster towns.

- Outside of the lands of the earldom, the Church in the rest of Ulster remained under the control of Gaelic bishops and abbots. Many of these continued to lead worldly lives.

ACTIVITIES

Complete the following sentences:
(a) After 1300 farming in Ireland changed as corn-growing was replaced more and more by _____.
(b) The Gaelic kingdom of Ulaid was situated in _____.
(c) Carrickfergus Castle was founded by _____.
(d) Town dwellers in medieval Ulster earned their living by _____.
(e) John de Courcy founded Cistercian abbeys at _____.

True or false?
(a) A betagh was a type of Norman soldier.
(b) John de Courcy captured the Gaelic McDunlevy kingdom.
(c) The people of Carrickfergus traded with France during the Middle Ages.
(d) The friars set up monasteries in lonely parts of the countryside.
(e) The Normans had difficulty attracting large numbers of settlers to Ulster.

Imagine that you were present during an attack on Carrickfergus Castle during the Middle Ages. Using the illustration of the castle as a guide, describe the activities of both the attackers and the defenders.

Write a paragraph on the achievements of John de Courcy, the Norman conqueror of Ulster.

THE NORMANS IN CONTROL

CONQUERING NEW TERRITORIES

While John de Courcy and his followers were carving out a province for themselves in Ulster other Norman warriors were capturing vast stretches of land in Munster, Leinster and Connaught. To this day we can still see the evidence of this in *mottes* or artificial hills scattered throughout the country. On these the Norman conquerors built hastily constructed wooden castles. Often they were surrounded by an enclosed space known as a *bailey*. Archaeologists have discovered that, as well as building mottes on new sites, the Normans often built their wooden castles on the sites of earlier Celtic ringforts. Most of these mottes were constructed between 1170 and 1230.

The principal Norman families in Ireland.

A reconstructi of an early Norman motte

In the larger towns most of the mottes were replaced by stone castles. For example, at Athlone, Co. Westmeath, an important crossing point of the river Shannon, a large stone castle was built around 1210 to replace an earlier motte. However, sometimes even in towns mottes were not covered with stone castles. Even today an early Norman motte called 'Millmount' can still be seen overlooking the town of Drogheda.

The Millmount, Drogheda.

In Munster Norman families such as the Fitzgeralds, the Barrys and the Roches gained control over much of Waterford, Cork and Kerry. The Fitzgeralds later became the rich and powerful earls of Desmond, controlling a vast area of land stretching from west Kerry to Waterford.

In Tipperary and Kilkenny Theobald Walter, the ancestor of the Butler family, was granted land by Prince John, Henry II's son. The Butlers later became earls of Ormond, where they ruled over most of Tipperary and Kilkenny from their headquarters at Kilkenny Castle.

In Connaught the main family of Norman conquerors was called de Burgo which later changed to Burke. As well as conquering most of Galway, Mayo and Sligo the de Burgos set up towns in Galway and Athenry. However, as in Ulster, very few English tenants arrived in Connaught and most of the conquered land was worked by Irish tenants.

Having conquered large areas of Ireland it was necessary for the kings of England and their followers to organise a system of defence. One of the earliest rulers to plan this was Prince John, a son of Henry II who was made lord of Ireland by his father in 1177.

Kilkenny Castle.

Irish towns built or developed by the Normans.

- Coleraine
- Carrickfergus
- Sligo
- Dundalk
- Kells
- Navan
- Drogheda
- Galway
- Athenry
- Athlone
- Dublin
- Loughrea
- Roscrea
- Kildare
- Nenagh
- Thurles
- Carlow
- Limerick
- Cashel
- Kilkenny
- Carrick-on-Suir
- Tralee
- Clonmel
- New Ross
- Wexford
- Dungarvan
- Waterford
- Cork
- Youghal
- Kinsale

The remains of the Norman castle at Athenry, Co. Galway.

KING JOHN IN IRELAND

Prince John first arrived in Ireland in 1185 with a force of over 2,000 soldiers. He ordered the construction of several castles as a protection for the Norman conquests. One of the largest of these at Limerick city is still known as King John's Castle. John also made grants of land to his followers, either of territory that had still to be conquered or of lands which had belonged to the earliest conquerors such as Strongbow or Fitzstephen, who were dead by this time.

After he became king in 1199 on the death of his elder brother, Richard I, John once more turned his attention to Ireland. He was very suspicious of the powerful Norman lords in Ireland and wished to replace them with men more dependent on him. In particular he resented the power of the earl of Ulster, John de Courcy, and resolved to remove him from that position. John declared war on de Courcy and took away his title as earl in 1205. De Courcy was captured, imprisoned and finally pardoned. After this he left Ireland and returned to live in England. In his place King John appointed Hugh de Lacy, a younger brother of Walter de Lacy, earl of Meath. Hugh de Lacy was to remain earl of Ulster until his death in 1243.

King John's Castle, Limerick.

King John paid a second visit to Ireland in 1210. On this occasion he ordered that the eastern part of the country be divided into twelve counties or shires, each with its own sheriff and court. This was an important improvement in the government of the Norman colony in Ireland.

However, after this visit of King John in 1210 it would be almost 200 years before another king of England visited his Irish lordship. In the absence of such visits the English lordship was ruled by the king's representative, the lord deputy.

King John hunting as shown in a medieval manuscript.

TEST YOUR KNOWLEDGE
1 *Explain the terms 'motte' and 'bailey'.*
2 *Name two Norman families which gained land in Munster.*
3 *Name the families who were*
   (a) earls of Desmond
   (b) earls of Ormond
4 *Name one castle in Ireland founded by King John.*
5 *What happened to John de Courcy in 1205?*
6 *Name one reform implemented by King John on his visit to Ireland in 1210.*

THE LORD DEPUTY

The lord deputy was directly appointed by the king to rule over the part of Ireland controlled by the Normans. Sometimes the king appointed a powerful Norman lord to this position. We have seen already how the first lord deputy was Hugh de Lacy, earl of Meath, appointed by Henry II in 1172. Later on in the Middle Ages nobles with large Irish territories, such as the earl of Ormond or the earl of Desmond, were appointed lord deputy.

At other times the king appointed Englishmen as lord deputy. These usually came to Ireland for a few years and then returned to England when their term of office was up. From time to time the king would appoint one of his own sons to take charge in Ireland. Henry II appointed his son, Prince John, as lord deputy in 1177 and nearly 200 years later Edward III (1327-77) appointed one of his sons. This was Lionel, duke of Clarence, appointed in 1361 because he had succeeded to the vast lands of the earl of Ulster by marrying Elizabeth, daughter of William de Burgo, the earl of Ulster who had been murdered in 1333.

Whether a Norman lord, an English official or a royal prince, the work of a lord deputy remained the same. His main task was to lead the king's army in Ireland and to protect his territories from attack by the Gaelic Irish. English settlers in town and countryside were under constant threat of attack. Even Dublin, the capital city, was threatened. On Easter Monday in the year 1209 hundreds of citizens were surprised while at play and killed by the O'Tooles and O'Byrnes at Cullensword, south of Dublin. To protect the Norman areas from such attacks the lord deputy was entitled to levy taxes to pay his army.

As well as fighting against his king's enemies the lord deputy was in charge of the government of the country. His headquarters were at Dublin Castle, which also housed departments of State like the exchequer or finance office and the chancery where all records of government were kept. Some of these records have survived and give us an insight into the government of the various deputies.

The lord deputy was also in charge of the system of justice. As the chief judge he could pardon anybody in the king's name. Indeed, he frequently travelled around the country holding law courts in various towns.

Dublin Castle.

A medieval picture of people counting money in the Exchequer.

THE COUNCIL AND THE PARLIAMENT

To assist the lord deputy in governing the country there was a small group of men known as the *council*. These were usually rich and powerful lords and bishops. Some members of the council had special functions, such as the treasurer who was in charge of tax-raising and the department of the exchequer. The *chancellor* was another important member of the council. He was usually a bishop, and his function was to take charge of the chancery where government documents were kept, together with royal seals or stamping moulds which gave the king's approval to important letters.

As in England, a parliament developed in Ireland before 1300. The first important gathering of the Irish parliament for which we have a record was in 1297. Its members included bishops and abbots, lay lords such as earls and barons and elected members for the various towns and counties under English control.

As the lord deputy frequently travelled from place to place, the parliament also moved. Although it usually met in Dublin it also held meetings in towns such as Drogheda, Kilkenny, Naas, Trim and Castle-dermot. The main function of the parliament was to pass laws and to raise taxes, both for the upkeep of the Norman colony in Ireland and for passing on to the king of England.

1   *How was the lord deputy appointed?*
2   *What were the main functions carried out by the lord deputy?*
3   *Name two departments of the lord deputy's government.*
4   *What powers did he have over the courts?*
5   *Explain the function of the council.*
6   *Name one member of the council and explain his work.*
7   *What were the principal tasks carried out by the parliament in medieval Ireland?*

IRELAND AND ENGLAND UNDER THE NORMANS

Various kings of England were concerned to raise as much tax as possible in Ireland. For a few generations after the Norman conquest there were close links between England and the Normans living in Ireland. These links included loyalty to the same king; similar laws; trade, which included imports and exports in both directions; and a shared common language, whether French or English. It was clear that both English kings and the English in Ireland regarded the country as an opportunity to increase their wealth. All were agreed in regarding the Gaelic Irish as barbarians and a threat to the well-being and prosperity of the English settlers in Ireland.

However, from around 1300 onwards matters began to change. More and more English settlers married Irish wives and their descendants spoke the Irish language and followed Irish customs. This was not surprising because the Normans were noted for their ability to adapt to new surroundings. In Italy they became Italian, in England they learnt the English language, and in Ireland many of them were becoming more Irish than the Irish themselves.

As part of this trend many Norman lords in Ireland began to make war on their neighbours, just like the Gaelic kings. By 1300 the king of England had become a remote figure indeed for many of the English living in the Irish towns and countryside.

Chapter 4: Review

- While de Courcy was capturing land in Ulster, other Norman lords were winning territories in Leinster, Munster and Connaught.

- When the Normans captured an area they usually built a motte and bailey and constructed wooden castles. These were later replaced by stone castles in important towns.

- In Munster the main Norman families were the Fitzgeralds, Barrys and Roches. The Fitzgeralds later became earls of Desmond.

- The Butler family gained control of Tipperary and Kilkenny. They later became earls of Ormond and ruled their vast lands from Kilkenny Castle.

In Connaught the principal family of Norman conquerors were the de Burgos who founded the towns of Galway and Athenry.

King John (1199-1216) paid two visits to Ireland. The first took place in 1185 when he was a prince and lord of Ireland. During this visit he ordered the construction of several castles.

During his second visit to Ireland in 1210 King John divided the areas under English control into shires or counties.

In 1205 King John removed John de Courcy from his position and created Hugh de Lacy earl of Ulster in his place.

The main governor of the English territories in Ireland was the lord deputy. He was appointed by the king and was in charge of an army to protect the territories from attack by the Gaelic Irish.

- The lord deputy was also in charge of the government of the country and was the chief judge. He frequently travelled around the land holding law courts in various towns.

- A council of powerful lords and bishops advised the lord deputy concerning his government of the king's lands.

- As in England there was a parliament in Ireland during the Middle Ages. It was called together by the lord deputy and its main functions were to pass laws and to raise taxes for the king.

- Most kings of England were mainly interested in Ireland as a source of taxes which they needed to finance their various wars.

- By 1300 many of the Normans in Ireland had adopted Gaelic customs of dress and behaviour and spoke the Irish language.

ACTIVITIES

1 *True or false?*
   (a) *The lord deputy was elected by the parliament.*
   (b) *The earl of Ormond was a member of the Butler family.*
   (c) *King John removed John de Courcy from his position as earl of Ulster in 1205.*
   (d) *The Fitzgeralds founded the towns of Galway and Athenry.*
   (e) *A motte was an artificial hill on which a castle was built.*

2 *Complete the following sentences:*
   (a) *The earls of Desmond belonged to a Norman family called _____.*
   (b) *By 1300 many English settlers in Ireland had _____.*
   (c) *The king's representative in Ireland was called _____.*
   (d) *His headquarters were situated at _____.*
   (e) *The principal functions of the parliament in medieval Ireland were _____.*

3 *Write a short account on the activities of King John in Ireland both before and after he became king.*

4 *Draw a map of Ireland and include the following:*
   (a) *The principal Norman towns.*
   (b) *The main Norman families and the areas which they conquered.*

THE DECLINE OF THE NORMAN COLONY IN IRELAND AND THE GAELIC REVIVAL

THE BRUCE INVASION

On 25 May 1315 Edward Bruce, the brother of the king of Scotland, landed in Larne harbour, Co. Antrim with an army of over 6,000 soldiers. For over three years his army was to march throughout Ireland causing widespread havoc and destruction, especially to the towns and countryside occupied by the Normans.

In the previous year Robert Bruce had won a crushing victory over King Edward II of England at the Battle of Bannockburn in Scotland. This enabled Bruce to extend his war against England by getting his brother to attack the English lordship in Ireland. The Bruces hoped to cut off supplies of corn and money reaching England from Ireland.

Robert Bruce already had connections with Ireland. He was once an exile in Rathlin Island off the coast of Antrim, and he had married a daughter of Richard de Burgo, the red earl of Ulster. There were, in addition, traditional close links of trade and travel between Antrim and Down and the west coast of Ireland.

Soon after landing at Larne, Edward Bruce defeated local groups of Normans and was joined by a number of Gaelic rulers and their armies. He defeated an army of the earl of Ulster and forced him to retreat into Connaught. In May 1316, a year after his arrival in Ireland, Edward Bruce had himself crowned king of Ireland at Faughart near Dundalk in Co. Louth. However, Ireland was suffering from bad harvests and famine at the time and this, together with a Norman victory over the Irish at the Battle of Athenry, weakened the position of Edward Bruce.

In order to assist his brother, Robert Bruce himself landed at Carrickfergus early in 1317 with a huge army. Both brothers and their armies marched south in order to capture Dublin. The citizens of Dublin built a new wall and burned the suburbs as a means of defence. However, the Bruces bypassed Dublin and marched south into Kilkenny, Tipperary and Limerick. The Scots plundered and destroyed crops and houses everywhere they marched. On learning of the arrival of English reinforcements they retreated into Ulster, where Edward remained after Robert returned to Scotland.

The Bruce
invasion of
Ireland.

Both sides in the war appealed to Pope John XXII for his support. While the pope condemned Bruce and the others engaged in rebellion he also urged King Edward II to govern Ireland more justly.

As long as he remained in Ulster, Edward Bruce was fairly secure. However, late in 1318 he marched southwards again, and on 14 October 1318 his 3,000-strong army of Scots and Irish was defeated by a much larger English army at Faughart, Co. Louth. Ironically this was the very spot where he had earlier been crowned king of Ireland. Edward Bruce himself and about two-thirds of his followers were killed in the battle.

The Bruce invasion had inflicted serious damage on the English colony in Ireland. Indeed, so great was the damage caused that the Gaelic Irish who had welcomed Bruce were glad to see him defeated. At the same time as the invasion, there were serious crop failures and famines throughout the country. These merely marked the beginning of a long period of difficulty for the English in Ireland. The next serious blow which they suffered was even worse than the Bruce invasion: the worst of all medieval plagues, the Black Death.

TEST YOUR KNOWLEDGE
1. *Where and when did Edward Bruce land in Ireland?*
2. *Name the famous battle in which Robert Bruce defeated the English in 1314.*
3. *What was the main reason for the Bruce invasion of Ireland?*
4. *What event took place at Faughart, Co. Louth in May 1316?*

37

5 *Describe the response of the citizens of Dublin to the threat from the Bruce forces.*

6 *How did the Scots troops behave in their marches through Ireland?*

7 *Where was Edward Bruce finally defeated in October 1318?*

THE BLACK DEATH

This dreaded killer plague reached Europe from China in 1347. Humans caught the disease when they were bitten by the infected fleas living on black rats. In the dirty conditions of medieval towns and cities it spread rapidly. Entire families often died from the plague. It reached Ireland in the summer of 1348.

In Ireland the Black Death killed many more people among the Normans than among the Gaelic Irish. This was because the Normans lived in village communities in the countryside or in the densely populated towns. The Gaelic Irish who lived in scattered communities in the countryside escaped more lightly. It has been estimated that about one-third of the English population in Ireland was wiped out by the Black Death.

A medieval manuscript showing a procession of people praying for an end to the Black Death.

Although the major epidemic passed after a few years, plague returned at regular intervals for the rest of the Middle Ages. The huge decline in the population was a major cause of weakness in the English colony in Ireland and an encouragement to the Gaelic rulers to continue their attacks.

WORKING WITH EVIDENCE

At the time of the Black Death in Ireland, a member of the Dominican Order in Kilkenny, Friar John Clyn, wrote an account of the events taking place all around him. He himself died of the plague. Read the following extract from the account of Friar Clyn and answer the questions which follow.

This pestilence was so contagious that those who touched the dead or persons sick of the plague were straightaway infected themselves, and died, so that the confessor and his penitent were carried to the same grave.

And from very fear and horror men were seldom brave enough to perform works of mercy, such as visiting the sick and burying the dead.

For many died from boils and ulcers and running sores which grew on the legs and beneath the armpits, whilst other suffered pains in the head and went almost into a frenzy, whilst others spat blood.

There was hardly a house in which one only had died, but as a rule man and wife and the children went the common way of death.

How do we know that the plague was highly contagious?
What danger did priests face while hearing confessions?
Why did people stop visiting the sick and burying the dead?
How did Friar Clyn describe the outward signs of the plague?
Once the Black Death entered a house, what was the usual outcome?

THE GAELIC REVIVAL AND THE STATUTES OF KILKENNY

From as early as 1250 onwards Gaelic rulers in various parts of Ireland had begun to recover lands which their ancestors had lost to the Normans. In 1261 the McCarthy family drove the Normans out of a large part of Kerry; in 1270 many Norman settlers were removed from Connaught by the O'Connors. Even in Leinster, the province most under Norman control, Gaelic rulers began to put pressure on the lands occupied by the Normans.

As well as attack from the outside, some of the Norman customs were a source of their weakness. We have seen earlier how many settlers began to use the Irish language, Irish dress and customs. They also frequently used the Brehon laws instead of the English common law. In addition to this, some of the main Norman territories, such as the province of Leinster and the earldom of Meath, were divided up between daughters when their owners died without sons.

Norman knights like the de Burgos of Connaught became more Irish than the Irish themselves.

One of the worst disasters to occur in a Norman territory happened in the earldom of Ulster in 1333. In that year the 'brown earl', William de Burgo, was murdered by one of his own followers near Belfast. His lands and titles passed through his daughter Elizabeth to her husband, Prince Lionel, duke of Clarence, and eventually to the king of England. Although the king's officials governed the earldom of Ulster after the earl's death, more and more land was recaptured by Gaelic rulers. The English settlers, reduced in number by the Black Death and other plagues, were in a weak position to resist. As a result between 1300 and 1450 the Gaelic Irish regained control of four-fifths of the earldom of Ulster.

The position in Ulster had parallels in the rest of the country. The Gaelic rulers began to recruit mercenary soldiers known as *gallowglasses* from Scotland to help them in their attacks on the English settlements. By 1366 the king's government was so alarmed that a parliament meeting in Kilkenny passed the famous *Statutes of Kilkenny* in an effort to halt the Gaelic revival.

WORKING WITH EVIDENCE

Read the following introduction to the Statutes of Kilkenny and answer the questions which follow.

Whereas at the conquest of the land of Ireland and for a long time afterwards, the English of the said land used the English language, mode of riding and of dress and were governed according to the English law – now many English of the said land, forsaking the English language, manners and mode of riding, laws and usages, live and govern themselves according to the manners, fashion and language of the Irish enemies, and also have made several marriages and alliances between themselves and the Irish enemies, where the said land and people, the English language, the allegiance due to our lord the king, and the English laws are put into subjection and decayed, and the Irish enemies exalted and raised up contrary to reason.

1 *How did the English settlers behave for a long time after the conquest?*
2 *What type of law did they use?*
3 *By 1366 what way were many of the English settlers behaving?*
4 *What was the attitude of the parliament to the Gaelic Irish?*
5 *Did many English settlers abandon their loyalty to the king?*
6 *What was the principal complaint of the authors?*

According to the Statutes of Kilkenny the English settlers were forbidden to marry the Gaelic Irish or to send their children to be fostered among them. They were to use English and not Brehon laws and were not allowed sell horses or weapons to the Gaelic Irish. They were to speak English, use English surnames and follow English customs. They were also forbidden to play hurling and encouraged to learn the use of bows and arrows instead!

Gallowglasses.

The Statutes of Kilkenny did nothing to halt the decline of the Norman colony and the spread of the Gaelic revival. Indeed, a year later the new lord deputy was none other than Gerald, earl of Desmond, also known as Gearóid Iarla, a famous author of poems in the Irish language. In one poem he called the Irish his kinsmen and declared:

> I prefer being with my kinsmen
> Though they intend to plunder me
> Than to be chained in prison
> By the saxon king in London.

Conditions went from bad to worse for the king's government in Ireland until eventually the king himself, Richard II, decided to visit the country in 1394.

KING RICHARD II IN IRELAND

In September 1394 Richard II landed in Waterford with an army of 10,000 men. He was the first monarch to visit his Irish lordship since King John in 1210. This was by far the largest army to appear in Ireland during the Middle Ages. One by one the Gaelic kings submitted to him and promised to remain loyal. Richard returned to England in May 1395, well satisfied with his expedition.

No sooner had he returned home than the Gaelic kings broke out again in rebellion. In 1398 the lord deputy himself, Robert Mortimer, earl of March, King Richard's cousin and heir, was killed in a battle against the O'Byrnes of Wicklow. King Richard once more set sail for Ireland, arriving at Waterford in June 1399. However, his army suffered heavy casualties in clashes against MacMurrough of Leinster. Suddenly news arrived that the king's cousin, Henry, duke of Lancaster, had taken

King Richard II landing in Ireland.

over the kingdom. Richard hastily returned to England, where he was removed from power and eventually murdered in prison. He had completely failed in his aim of reversing the tide of the Gaelic revival in Ireland. Rather than being reversed, it was to continue for the following century.

THE RISE OF THE GREAT LORDS

Between 1400 and 1500 the area under English rule in Ireland continued to decline. Eventually the king's authority was only recognised in the towns and in an area around Dublin known as the *Pale*. In Ulster only the eastern part of Co. Down remained of the

The map shows the area of the Pale around 1500. Part of it was enclosed by a deep ditch.

A tower house in Clonfert, Co. Galway, one of many such fortresses built throughout Ireland from 1400 onwards as the king's rule grew weaker.

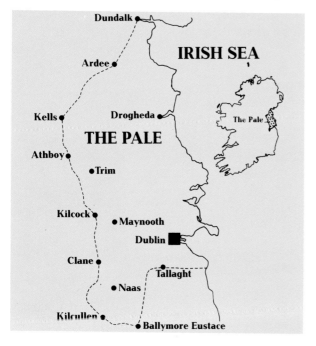

extensive earldom of Ulster. The rest of the land had been conquered by Gaelic rulers, especially the O'Neills of Clandeboy, relations of the O'Neills of Tyrone.

As the power of the king decreased that of the great lords increased. The most powerful of these were the earls of Kildare and the earls of Desmond, members of the Fitzgerald family, and the Butler earls of Ormond. The lord deputy was usually chosen from one of these three earls. They possessed armies of their own and frequently made alliances with the Gaelic rulers.

By 1450 it appeared that the power of the king of England in Ireland was going to remain weak. All of this was to change, however, after a strong and determined royal family came to power in England in 1485: the *Tudors*.

Outside and inside views of the Butler residence at Carrick-on-Suir, Co. Waterford.

Gaelic
Anglo-Norman

The ruling Gaelic and Norman families in Ireland around 1500.

43

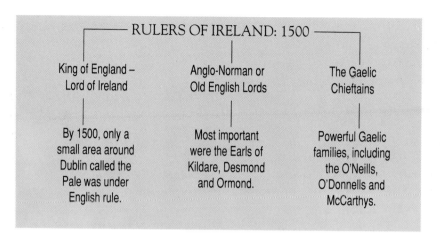

RULERS OF IRELAND: 1500

King of England – Lord of Ireland	Anglo-Norman or Old English Lords	The Gaelic Chieftains
By 1500, only a small area around Dublin called the Pale was under English rule.	Most important were the Earls of Kildare, Desmond and Ormond.	Powerful Gaelic families, including the O'Neills, O'Donnells and McCarthys.

TEST YOUR KNOWLEDGE
1   *List three important rules from the Statutes of Kilkenny.*
2   *Were these laws a success? Explain your answer.*
3   *Who was Gearóid Iarla?*
4   *What was the result of Richard II's first visit to Ireland (1394)?*
5   *Why did the king return in 1399?*
6   *Why did he hasten back to England?*
7   *Explain the term 'Pale'.*
8   *Name the royal family which came to power in England in 1485.*

Chapter 5: Review

- In 1315 Edward Bruce, the brother of King Robert Bruce of Scotland, began an invasion of Ireland when he landed in Larne, Co. Antrim with a army of 6,000 men.

- The Bruce invasion had the aim of preventing supplies of corn and money reaching the king of England from Ireland.

- For over three years, Bruce's army was to march throughout Ireland causing widespread havoc and destruction.

- In May 1316 Edward Bruce had himself crowned king of Ireland at Faughart near Dundalk in Co. Louth.

- Early in 1317 King Robert Bruce landed at Carrickfergus with an army to join his brother's campaign. Together they marched on Dublin but by-passed it when they saw it well defended.

- After a campaign of widespread destruction in Munster the Bruces returned to Ulster. Edward remained there while Robert returned to Scotland.

- In October 1318 Edward Bruce was defeated and killed at Faughart, Co. Louth by an army of English settlers. His invasion, though it ended in failure, had caused widespread destruction and had greatly weakened the English colony in Ireland.

- In 1348 another disaster struck Ireland: the killer plague known as the Black Death. It wiped out a vast number of people and it had a worse impact on the English in towns and countryside than on the Gaelic Irish.

From around 1250 onwards Gaelic rulers had begun to recapture land from the Normans. Norman settlers began to adopt Gaelic customs and speak the Irish language.

The Statutes of Kilkenny (1367) were aimed at preventing the English in Ireland from adopting the Gaelic way of life. They failed by and large to prevent this happening.

In 1394 King Richard II arrived in Ireland with an army of 10,000 men. He was the first king of England to visit Ireland since King John in 1210.

During Richard's visit the Gaelic rulers submitted to him and promised to remain loyal. Immediately he left for England they once more made war on the English colony.

- After the death in battle of the lord deputy and Richard's heir, Roger Mortimer, the king returned to Ireland in 1399. This time many Gaelic rulers refused to submit but he had to hasten back to England where he was removed from power and eventually murdered.

- Between 1400 and 1500 the area of Ireland under English rule continued to decline. Eventually it only included the main towns and an area around Dublin known as the Pale.

- While the power of the king declined the power of the Gaelic kings and the Norman lords increased throughout Ireland.

ACTIVITIES

Fill in the blanks with the words from the box.

Scotland	Ulster	Edward	Gaelic	defeated	Normans	Ireland	colony	destruction

In May 1315 _____ Bruce, the brother of the king of _____, landed in Larne harbour. He defeated local groups of _____ and was joined by a number of rulers. He defeated an army of the earl of _____ and forced him to retreat into Connaught. In May 1316 he had himself crowned king of _____ near Dundalk. Over two years later, he was _____ in battle by an army of English settlers. His invasion had caused widespread _____ and greatly weakened the English _____ in Ireland.

True or false?
(a) The Black Death killed more in the Gaelic Irish areas than in the English colony.
(b) The Statutes of Kilkenny were almost a complete failure.
(c) Between 1300 and 1450 the Gaelic rulers regained control of four-fifths of the earldom of Ulster.
(d) A gallowglass was a peasant working on the land.
(e) Richard II was killed in Ireland in 1399.

Imagine that you were an official working for the earl of Ulster at the time of the Bruce invasion. Write an account of this event from your point of view.

List the main reasons for the passing of the Statutes of Kilkenny.

Write a paragraph on the visits of King Richard II to Ireland.

IRELAND UNDER THE EARLY TUDORS: 1485-1558

HENRY VII (1485-1509), KING OF ENGLAND AND LORD OF IRELAND

When the first Tudor, Henry VII, became king of England in 1485, he became lord of Ireland as well.

His first concern was to secure his position in England. In the beginning of his reign, Henry paid little attention to Ireland and was quite happy to leave the country in the care of his lord deputy. At this time the lord deputy of Ireland was Garret Mór Fitzgerald, earl of Kildare and the most powerful man in the country.

Henry VII of England.

GARRET MÓR FITZGERALD, EARL OF KILDARE: 'THE GREAT EARL'

Garret Mór was a member of the powerful Anglo-Norman Fitzgerald family which had vast lands in Kildare, Carlow and Wicklow. He ruled over his huge estate from his great stone castle at Maynooth with the help of his own private army. While many people feared 'the great earl', Garret was careful to build up friendships or alliances with many of the Gaelic and Anglo-Norman Lords, through marriages, for example.

From 1477 onwards Garret Mór was the king's lord deputy in Ireland. During the War of the Roses in England, Garret Mór and the Fitzgeralds supported the Yorkist side. When Henry Tudor of the house of Lancaster became king in 1485, he could not remove his powerful and influential lord deputy.

Garret Mór continued to support the Yorkist enemies of Henry VII. In 1487 he upheld the claims of the pretender, Lambert Simnel, who was crowned king at Christchurch Cathedral in Dublin. This greatly angered Henry VII. A second pretender, Perkin Warbeck, arrived in

Ireland in 1491. Although Garret Mór did not actively support him, he did not try to stop him. Henry VII was now determined to remove Garret from his position as lord deputy. In 1494 the earl of Kildare was dismissed and an Englishman, Sir Edward Poynings (1459-1521), was appointed in his place.

TEST YOUR KNOWLEDGE
1 When Henry VII became king of England in 1485, what Irish title did he also have?
2 Who was Garret Mór?
3 What lands did he rule over and where was his castle?
4 How did he build up alliances with other lords?
5 What position did Garret Mór hold from 1477 onwards?
6 Which side did he support in the Wars of the Roses?
7 Name the two Yorkist pretenders who went to Ireland.
8 Why do you think Garret Mór was dismissed from his position as lord deputy in 1494?

POYNINGS IN IRELAND

The new lord deputy, Sir Edward Poynings, arrived in Ireland with a large army in October 1494. He immediately called a meeting of the Irish parliament in Drogheda. Here Garret Mór was accused of treason. He was arrested and sent as a prisoner to London.

The parliament passed a number of laws, including one which ordered the strengthening of defences around the Pale. The most important act passed by this parliament became known as *Poynings' Law*.

Poynings' Law reduced the power of the Irish lord deputy and parliament in two ways:

The Irish parliament could not meet without the permission of the king of England and his council.
The Irish parliament could not pass any laws until they were first approved by the king and his council in England.

Although Poynings' Law strengthened the rule of the king of England in Ireland, Henry VII soon realised that he still needed Garret Mór to keep the country in order. While the earl of Kildare was a prisoner in London, Gaelic chieftains seized the opportunity to attack the Pale. Henry VII was faced with the choice of sending a large and expensive English army to Ireland or reappointing Garret Mór as lord deputy. The king could not afford such an expedition so he released Garret Mór and sent him home to Ireland as lord deputy in 1496. Henry remarked at the time about Garret Mór: 'If all Ireland cannot rule this man, then he must rule Ireland.'

Garret Mór remained as lord deputy of Ireland until his death in 1513. He was succeeded by his son, Garret Óg (1487-1534).

TEST YOUR KNOWLEDGE
1 *Who arrived in Ireland as lord deputy in October 1494?*
2 *Where did the Irish parliament meet?*
3 *What action did parliament take against Garret Mór?*
4 *Explain how Poynings' Law reduced the power of the Irish lord deputy and parliament.*
5 *Why did Henry VII decide to reappoint Garret Mór as lord deputy in 1496?*
6 *When did Garret Mór die? Who succeeded him as lord deputy of Ireland?*

GARRET ÓG FITZGERALD, EARL OF KILDARE

Before the death of Garret Mór, a new king of England, Henry VIII, had come to power in 1509. Henry VIII was much more secure on the throne of England than his father had been. He was a strong, forceful king who did not want any of the lords in Ireland to become too powerful. He took a close interest in Ireland as he knew that his enemies in Europe might use the country as a backdoor to England. After Garret Óg became lord deputy in 1513, Henry VIII did not allow him to have the same power as his father.

By 1530 Garret Óg's enemies in England had become very powerful. The Butlers, earls of Ormond, were traditional enemies of the Fitzgerald earls of Kildare. When Anne Boleyn, a member of the Butler family, became Henry VIII's second wife, Garret Óg's difficulties were increased.

In 1533 Garret Óg was called to London and placed in the Tower. This was the beginning of the end in the powerful Fitzgeralds of Kildare in Ireland.

Henry VIII of England.

Garret Óg, Ea of Kildare (1487-1534).

SILKEN THOMAS AND THE FALL OF THE HOUSE OF KILDARE

When Garret Óg was called to London in 1533 he left his young son, Thomas (1513-37) in charge in Ireland. Because of his rich clothes, he was known as Silken Thomas.

Thomas was a rash and quick-tempered young man. Knowing this, his father, Garret Óg, had warned him to take the advice of the council in Dublin in case of any emergency. Silken Thomas did not follow his father's instructions, however.

While Garret Óg was in London, his enemies in Ireland spread a false report that he had been put to death by Henry VIII. Before waiting to check on the truth of the story, Silken Thomas rashly began a rebellion against the king. He stormed into a meeting of the council which was taking place at St Mary's Abbey in Dublin. As he flung his sword of state, the symbol of the king's authority, to the ground, Silken Thomas swore that he would never again serve King Henry VIII.

Silken Thomas refusing to serve King Henry VIII at a meeting of the Council of State in St Mary's Abbey in Dublin, in June 1534.

The ruins of Maynooth Castle.

Although Thomas sent appeals for help to the pope and other Catholic rulers in Europe, he received no assistance from abroad.

Henry VIII soon sent a powerful army to Ireland under a new English-born lord deputy called Skeffington. The kings's army destroyed Maynooth Castle with cannon. Although those defending the castle surrendered, they were all executed. This incident became known as the *Pardon of Maynooth*.

Within two years the rebellion of the Fitzgeralds of Kildare was completely crushed. Henry VIII was determined to wipe out the Kildare family. Silken Thomas and his five uncles were executed at Tyburn in London in February 1537. Meanwhile Garret Óg, the last earl of Kildare, had died in despair in the Tower of London. Henry VIII took control of the Fitzgeralds' huge estates and added them to the Pale. The power and splendour of the mighty house of Kildare had disappeared for ever.

TEST YOUR KNOWLEDGE
1 *Why did Henry VIII wish to increase his power in Ireland?*
2 *How did Henry VIII try to limit the power of Garret Óg?*
3 *Who were the enemies of Garret Óg?*
4 *What happened to Garret Óg in 1513?*
5 *Who was Silken Thomas? Why did he rebel against Henry VIII?*
6 *What happened when Silken Thomas stormed into a meeting of the council in Dublin?*
7 *Name the lord deputy sent by Henry VIII to crush the rebellion.*
8 *What was the Pardon of Maynooth?*

HENRY VIII BRINGS THE REFORMATION TO IRELAND

By this time Henry VIII had made himself head of the Church in England. He then turned his attention to Ireland in order to do the same there. In 1536 he called the Irish parliament together in Dublin. Many members of parliament, especially the Old English lords of the Pale, did not want to deny the authority of the pope and make Henry the head of the Church. However, they were frightened by the ruthless crushing of the rebellion of Silken Thomas. The parliament passed the Act of Supremacy, recognising Henry as head of the Church in Ireland. In future, all those in high government positions would have to take an oath swearing this: *the oath of supremacy*.

A new religion was now set up in Ireland called the Church of Ireland. It was the State religion under the king's authority. No other religion was to be allowed to operate in the country. The parliament which brought in these changes became known as the Reformation parliament.

It was easy for Henry VIII to get laws passed making himself head of the Church in Ireland. It would be much harder to get the people of the country to accept the changes. Most people continued to remain loyal to the pope. The Gaelic chieftains took no notice of the Reformation and most Old English lords in the Pale remained Catholics. Those who had taken the oath to the king later ignored it. Even in Dublin the Reformation made little headway.

As in England, Henry VIII was also determined to close down the monasteries in Ireland. He suspected the monks because of their

Nuns in the Pale are forced to hand over their convent to the king's soldiers.

loyalty to the pope and wished to take control of the riches of the monasteries.

By 1541 all the monasteries in the Pale and in the towns under English control had been closed down. Henry VIII took over their land and sold it to local lords.

Most of the monasteries in Gaelic Ireland remained open under the protection of Gaelic chieftains. Some of them were not closed down until after 1600 when English power spread over the whole country.

TEST YOUR KNOWLEDGE
1 *Why was the Irish parliament called together in 1536?*
2 *Why did many Old English lords support Henry VIII's religious changes?*
3 *What was the Act of Supremacy?*
4 *By what name did the parliament of 1536 become known?*
5 *What was the attitude of the people in Gaelic areas to the Reformation?*
6 *Why did Henry VIII wish to close the monasteries in Ireland?*
7 *What happened to the monasteries in the areas controlled by the Gaelic chieftains?*

THE REIGN OF EDWARD VI (1547-53)

King Edward VI (1547-53).

By Henry VIII's death in 1547 the Reformation had made little progress in Ireland, apart from the closing of the monasteries. Henry VIII had kept the mass and the Catholic sacraments. Under his young son, Edward VI, an attempt was made to introduce Protestant teachings and services to Ireland.

51

Archbishop Browne of Dublin tried hard to introduce Protestant services in Ireland. However, most Irish bishops refused to follow his lead. The Archbishop of Armagh left the country, saying that he would never be a bishop where the mass was not allowed.

The ordinary people were completely opposed to the changes in religion under Edward VI. Protestant bishops like John Bale of Ossory (Kilkenny) were only kept in power by the government's authority; otherwise they would have been expelled from their churches.

The short reign of Edward VI came to an end in 1553. He was succeeded by his Catholic half-sister, Queen Mary I, also known as Mary Tudor.

QUEEN MARY RESTORES THE CATHOLIC RELIGION

There was widespread rejoicing in Ireland in 1553 when news arrived that the Catholic queen, Mary, had succeeded to the throne. In Kilkenny the people celebrated in the streets and in public houses. The town authorities gave permission for the mass to be said openly in the town's churches.

The new queen soon restored the Catholic religion and this was widely welcomed in Ireland. As in England, Queen Mary was unable to take back the monasteries from their new owners and return them to the monks.

English Protestants were persecuted during the reign of Mary Tudor, but the small number of Irish Protestants were not interfered with. Protestant bishops, however, lost their positions but were allowed to leave the country.

**Queen Mary Tudor
(1553-58).**

52

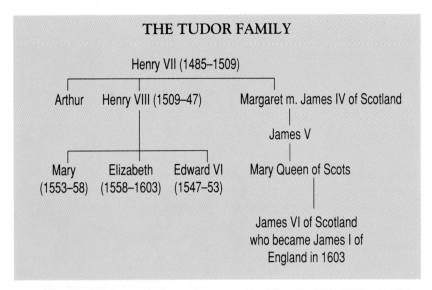

THE TUDOR FAMILY

Henry VII (1485–1509)

- Arthur
- Henry VIII (1509–47)
- Margaret m. James IV of Scotland

Henry VIII (1509–47):
- Mary (1553–58)
- Elizabeth (1558–1603)
- Edward VI (1547–53)

Margaret m. James IV of Scotland:
- James V
- Mary Queen of Scots
- James VI of Scotland who became James I of England in 1603

Although Mary's religious policies were largely welcomed in Ireland, she proved as determined as her father, Henry VIII, in extending English rule there. She was to use a new method to achieve this aim: *plantation*.

Chapter 6: Review

Garret Mór Fitzgerald was one of the most powerful men in Ireland. He owned a huge estate, had his own private army and was connected with both Gaelic and Anglo-Norman families through marriage alliances.

From 1477 onwards Garret Mór was the king's deputy in Ireland. He had supported the Yorkists in the Wars of the Roses but, when Henry Tudor of the house of Lancaster became King Henry VIII in 1485, Garret remained on as lord deputy. However, he supported the Yorkist pretenders, Lambert Simnel and Perkin Warbeck.

In 1494 the earl of Kildare was dismissed as lord deputy and an Englishman named Sir Edward Poynings was appointed in his place. He called a parliament in Drogheda which passed a law known as Poynings' Law. This stated that an Irish parliament could not meet without the king's permission and no laws could be passed without the king's approval.

- Poynings failed to keep law and order in the country and in 1496 Garret Mór was reappointed lord deputy. He held the position until his death in 1513, when he was replaced by his son, Garret Óg.

- From the beginning Garret Óg had many enemies who plotted to reduce his power, among them King Henry VIII, the Butlers and Anne Boleyn, second wife of Henry VIII and a member of the Butler family. Garret was often called to London to answer charges made against him.

- In 1533 Garret was called to London and left his young inexperienced son, Silken Thomas, in charge. When enemies of the Kildares spread a rumour that Garret Óg had been killed, Thomas rushed into revolt against the king and his government.

- The rebellion was a disaster and all surrendered when Lord Skeffington used cannon to bombard the Kildare stronghold in Maynooth. Thomas and his five uncles were executed, and Garret Óg died of a broken heart. The house of Kildare had been wiped out.

- In 1536 the Reformation parliament met in Dublin under the orders of Henry VIII. It passed the Act of Supremacy, making the king the head of the Church and ordering all holders of high government positions to take the oath of supremacy to the king.

- The Gaelic chieftains and their people ignored the changes of the Reformation and continued to practise the Catholic religion.

- As in England, Henry VIII ordered th[e] closing of the monasteries in Ireland. 1541 most monasteries in the Pale an[d] the towns had been closed. In the are[a] controlled by the Gaelic chieftains th[e] monasteries remained open. Some of these were not closed until after 160[0].

- During the reign of Edward V (1547-53) attempts were made to introduce Protestan[t] teachings and services to Ireland. Ho[w]ever, these failed, and most Irish peop[le] remained Catholics.

- Under Queen Mary I (1553-58) the Catholic religion was openly restored [in] Ireland. Unlike England where Protestants were persecuted, the smal[l] number of Irish Protestants were not harmed during Mary's reign.

ACTIVITIES

1 Complete each of the following sentences:
   (a) In 1485 a member of the Tudor family became king of England. He was known as _____.
   (b) In 1494 an Englishman replaced Garret Mór Fitzgerald as lord deputy. His name was _____.
   (c) The oath of supremacy was an oath recognising the king as _____.
   (d) The Pardon of Maynooth was _____.
   (e) When Henry VIII died in 1547, he was succeeded as ruler of England by _____.

2 Fact or opinion?
   Which of the following statements are facts and which are opinions?
   (a) Silken Thomas was right to rebel against Henry VIII.
   (b) By 1541 all the monasteries in the areas under English control in Ireland had been closed down.
   (c) Poynings' Law reduced the power of the Irish parliament.
   (d) Garret Mór Fitzgerald could have taken over complete power in Ireland.
   (e) Queen Mary Tudor restored the Catholic religion in England.

3 Write a paragraph on the rebellion of Silken Thomas and the fall of the house of Kildare.

4 Explain why the Reformation failed in Ireland under Henry VIII and Edward VI.

THE FIRST PLANTATIONS IN IRELAND

THE IDEA OF PLANTATIONS

English rulers looked to the American empires of Spain and Portugal as models for their future plans to rule Ireland. Thousands of Spanish and Portuguese settlers had emigrated to America, where they were given estates by their governments. In this way, they helped to maintain Spanish and Portuguese rule in these distant lands. From around 1540 onwards some rich and powerful men in England believed that their government should carry out plantations in Ireland. As the Old English and Gaelic Irish could not be trusted to support the king of England at all times, they believed that new English settlers loyal to the king should be brought over to Ireland. These would then be planted or settled on lands captured by the English.

The Reformation in England provided a great encouragement for those who believed in plantations in Ireland. Because most of the Gaelic Irish and Old English lords remained Catholic, English governments distrusted them and sought to introduce Protestant settlers in their place. Although the first plantation took place in Laois and Offaly under the Catholic queen, Mary Tudor, in 1556, all later plantations involved the arrival of Protestant settlers in Ireland. Let us now take a look at the earliest attempt introduce a plantation into Ireland.

n Mary Tudor
gland and
usband, King
p of Spain.

TEST YOUR KNOWLEDGE
1 What was a plantation?
2 How did the empires of Spain and Portugal provide English rulers with
   models?
3 Why were the Old English and Gaelic Irish not trusted by English rulers?
4 Explain how the Reformation in England encouraged those in favour of
   plantations in Ireland.

THE PLANTATION OF LAOIS AND OFFALY

Below we can see a picture of the busy town of Portlaoise today. In
the year 1556 it became the centre of the first plantation in Ireland.

In the land of Laois and Offaly, the Gaelic clans, the O'Moores and
the O'Connors, had continued to carry out raids at every opportunity.
Several English armies were sent to defeat them.

However, the Gaelic clans escaped by retreating into the safety of
the surrounding woods and bogs.

When Queen Mary Tudor became ruler of England in 1553, her
government decided to capture the lands of the O'Moores and the
O'Connors and to give them to English settlers.

The modern
town of
Portlaoise.

Irish clans such
as the O'Moore
and the
O'Connors
carried out
frequent raids
on the Pale.

56

THE SCHEME OF PLANTATION

Two-thirds of the land was taken from the native Irish and was to be 'planted' by English settlers. The remaining third – the worst land bordering the river Shannon – was set aside for the banished Irish, provided they remained loyal to the queen.

The English settlers had to build stone houses and keep armed followers in case of attack by the Gaelic clans.

Settlers were forbidden to mix in any way with the native Irish. They were not to marry into Irish families, to rent land to them or to hire them as servants.

The land taken over or confiscated by the English was *shired*, or divided up into counties. Laois became Queen's County, named after Queen Mary. Offaly was renamed King's County, after Mary's husband, King Philip II of Spain.

Each county had its own main town where the sheriff lived and where the courts were located. Maryborough (present-day Portlaoise) became the principal town in Queen's County. Philipstown (present-day Daingean) was the main town in King's County.

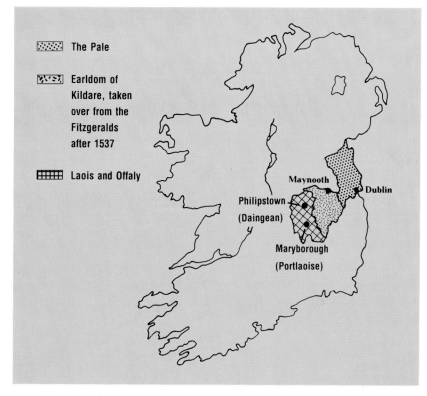

The Pale

Earldom of Kildare, taken over from the Fitzgeralds after 1537

Laois and Offaly

Maynooth

Dublin

Philipstown (Daingean)

Maryborough (Portlaoise)

e use of
ation, the
rs had
er extended
sh rule in
nd.

THE FIRST PLANTATION, SUCCESS OR FAILURE?

From the beginning the plantation of Laois and Offaly met with many difficulties. There were not enough English settlers to make the plantation a success. The O'Moores and the O'Connors were not easily defeated. They constantly attacked the new settlers, who lived in fear of raids by the Gaelic clans.

However, future English rulers learned a lot from the first plantation, and more successful plantations were later carried out in other parts of the country. The new approach, begun by Queen Mary, came to play a very important part in extending English rule throughout Ireland over the following hundred years.

TEST YOUR KNOWLEDGE
1 *What new policy was introduced by Queen Mary?*
2 *What Gaelic chieftains ruled over the lands of Laois and Offaly? In what way did they cause trouble for the English government?*
3 *How much of the land was given to new settlers?*
4 *What steps were taken to ensure that the settlers did not mix with the native Irish?*
5 *Name the new counties into which the land was divided.*
6 *How did the towns of Maryborough and Philipstown get their names?*
7 *Give two reasons why the plantation of Laois and Offaly was not a success.*

Chapter 7: Review

- A new approach to ruling Ireland was now developed by the English government. This involved removing the Gaelic clans from their lands and replacing them with loyal English settlers.

- English rulers looked to the empires of Spain and Portugal in America where thousands of settlers had successfully built up plantations on estates given to them by their governments.

- Because most of the Gaelic Irish and Old English lords remained Catholics, English governments distrusted them and preferred to introduce loyal Protestant English settlers.

- The first plantation in Ireland took place at Laois and Offaly during the reign of Queen Mary Tudor (1553-58

- It was carried out on lands confiscate from the Gaelic clans, the O'Moores and the O'Connors, who had constan attacked the Pale.

- Two-thirds of the land was set aside f English setters. The remaining one-third, worst land bordering on the river Shannon, was given to the native Iris

- English settlers had to build up stone houses and keep armed followers for protection. They were forbidden to m in any way with the native Irish.

The lands were divided into two counties. Laois became Queen's County after Queen Mary, and Offaly was known as King's County in honour of her husband, Philip of Spain.

Both counties had a main town: Maryborough (Portlaoise) in Laois and Philipstown (Daingean) in Offaly. Both of these towns contained forts and courthouses.

- The plantation of Laois and Offaly was not a success. There were not enough English settlers and the O'Moores and the O'Connors constantly attacked the plantation.

ACTIVITIES

Complete the following sentences:
(a) *The plan of introducing English settlers to take over the land captured from the Gaelic Irish was known as _____.*
(b) *The first plantation in Ireland was carried out during the reign of _____.*
(c) *This plantation took place in the land of _____, the home of the Irish clans, _____ and _____.*
(d) *To defend the plantation from attack, the English settlers were expected to build _____.*
(e) *The land taken over was 'shired'. This meant that _____.*

True or false?
State whether each of the following sentences is true or false.
(a) *English rulers got the idea of plantations from the Spanish and Portuguese settlements in the New World.*
(b) *The earliest plantation in Ireland took place in the lands of the defeated Fitzgerald family.*
(c) *English settlers were forbidden to mix with the native Irish.*
(d) *One of the main plantation towns, Philipstown, is the modern-day town of Portlaoise.*
(e) *The plantation of Laois and Offaly was very successful because the O'Moores and the O'Connors were completely defeated.*

Why do you think the English government decided on a policy of plantation in Ireland?

The following is an account written by an English lord deputy, St Leger, describing how English rule could be extended to Ireland. Read it carefully and answer the questions which follow.

The land of Ireland is very large, by estimations and description as large as England. In order to fill Ireland with new inhabitants, the numbers needed would be very large. Therefore, there is no prince who could spare so many subjects to depart out of his region, especially such people as would be suitable to inhabit another land. . . .

To bring about the local elimination and destruction of all Irishmen of the land would be very difficult indeed, considering the great hardness and misery these Irishmen can endure, more than the inhabitants of any other land. . . .

We therefore think that the easiest way is to accept the submission of those who have not offended seriously and to punish the leaders with all rigour and extremity. Having done this, we should keep garrisons of armed men in every part of the country to keep the Irish under control.

(a) Was the lord deputy's estimation of the size of Ireland accurate?
(b) What would be required 'in order to fill Ireland with new inhabitants'?
(c) Could any prince spare a large number of people to come to Ireland?
(d) Give one reason why the total destruction of the Gaelic Irish inhabitants would have been difficult.
(e) How did St Leger propose to treat those rebelling against the English government in Ireland?
(f) Explain the lord deputy's plan concerning garrisons.

IRELAND UNDER A NEW QUEEN

ELIZABETH I (1558-1603)

In November 1558 the twenty-five-year-old Princess Elizabeth succeeded her Catholic half-sister, Mary, as queen of England.

Like the other Tudor rulers before her, Elizabeth was determined to strengthen English power in Ireland and to extend her rule over the whole country.

From the start Elizabeth was at a disadvantage in Ireland because of lack of money. War was a very expensive business and Elizabeth's government was always short of money. The queen had to borrow huge amounts in order to conquer Ireland because she believed that this was essential for England's security. Foreign enemies like Spain could attempt to attack England through Ireland. Indeed, twice during Elizabeth's reign the king of Spain actually sent soldiers to help the Irish forces rebelling against the queen.

Besides war and conquest, the other main concern of Elizabeth I in Ireland was religion. As soon as she became queen she set about restoring the Protestant religion in England. Most English people at the time welcomed this. In Ireland conditions were completely different. Most Irish people had remained Catholics and had refused to support the attempts to bring in the Reformation under Henry VIII and Edward VI. Elizabeth I was not prepared to allow the Catholic religion in Ireland, however. She believed that all her subjects should be united in a single Church with herself at the head.

Queen Elizabeth I (1558-1603).

ELIZABETH I ESTABLISHES THE PROTESTANT CHURCH OF IRELAND AS THE STATE CHURCH

In 1560 the Irish parliament met in Dublin to pass new laws on religion in accordance with the queen's wishes. Great care was taken by government officials to ensure that those who opposed the Protestant religion were kept out of parliament. This parliament passed a number of important acts.

- *The Act of Supremacy.* This made the queen 'supreme governor of the Church of Ireland' and outlawed the authority of the pope. All holders of government positions would have to take an oath swearing to this, *the oath of supremacy.*
- *The Act of Uniformity.* This act stated that everyone should attend Sunday service in the local Protestant church. A fine of twelve pence was imposed on those refusing to attend. They became known as *recusants.* This act was new in Ireland. For the first time, penalties were imposed for refusal to attend Protestant services.

From 1560 the Protestant Church of Ireland under the rule of the queen was the official or State Church. All Irish people, including Catholics, had to pay taxes called *tithes* for the upkeep of its churches and the payment of its ministers. Its services were taken from the *Book of Common Prayer* as used in the Church of England. In the beginning these were supposed to be in Latin because most people in Ireland could not understand English.

The vast majority of people in Ireland would have nothing to do with Elizabeth's religion. In Gaelic areas and in the Anglo-Norman lordships, rich and poor alike remained Catholics. Even in the Pale and the English towns, very few people accepted the new religion. Almost twenty-five years after Elizabeth became queen, very little progress had

Trinity College, Dublin was founded by Queen Elizabeth I In 1591 on the site of the ruined Augustinian priory of All Hallows. The college was set up to spread the English language and the Protestant religion in Ireland.

been made. In 1574 a visitor found that there were practically no members of the State Church in Cork, only seven or eight in Limerick and about fifteen in Galway. Two years later a survey of the diocese of Meath revealed that, out of 224 parish churches, only fifteen had Protestant services.

The Church of Ireland was weakened from the start by a lack of suitable clergy. There were few properly educated Protestant ministers in the country. As well as this, most Irish people came to link the Protestant Church with English attempts to impose foreign rule on the country. While Elizabeth I was trying to impose her form of religion on Ireland, the Catholic Church was organising a revival in the country with the arrival of the *Counter-Reformation*.

TEST YOUR KNOWLEDGE
1   *How was the main aim of Elizabeth I in Ireland similar to that of other Tudor rulers?*
2   *Why was the queen willing to borrow large amounts of money to wage war in Ireland?*
3   *Why was Elizabeth I not prepared to allow the Catholic religion in Ireland?*
4   *Explain: (a) the Act of Supremacy; (b) the Act of Uniformity.*
5   *What were tithes and to whom were they paid?*
6   *How did most Irish people react to Elizabeth's religion?*
7   *State two reasons why the Protestant Church of Ireland failed to make progress in Ireland under Elizabeth.*

THE CATHOLIC COUNTER-REFORMATION IN IRELAND

By the time the Protestant religion became the State religion in Ireland in 1560, the Catholic Counter-Reformation was well under way on the continent. The *Council of Trent* had been meeting since 1545 and the Jesuits were sending missionaries all over Europe to fight the spread of Protestant teachings.

As early as 1542, a Jesuit mission consisting of three priests had arrived in Ireland. They remained for a short while, ministering to the people, and then reported back to Rome on the state of the Catholic religion in the country.

Many Catholic boys were first educated in small grammar schools in the towns and then sent to seminaries on the continent to train as priests. They were then smuggled back into the country where they celebrated mass in secret.

In 1560 the pope sent another Jesuit priest, Fr David Woulfe, to Ireland. He travelled around the country collecting information on the conditions of Catholics. He wrote about his experiences in a book called A *Description of Ireland*.

Ireland

Antwerp
Tournai • Louvain
Ypres • Douai
Rouen Lille
Paris Charleville
Boulay
Vassy
Bar-sur-Aube
Nantes
Poitiers
Bordeaux
Toulouse
Santiago
Valladolid
Salamanca
Alcalá
Madrid
Lisbon SPAIN
Seville
Prague
Viterbo
Rome

Irish colleges were founded in many towns on the continent of Europe where men studied to become priests from the time of Queen Elizabeth I onwards.

Fr Woulfe recommended various priests to the pope as suitable for promotion to bishops. One of these was Richard Creagh who was made archbishop of Armagh. However, Archbishop Creagh was captured in 1567 soon after his arrival in Ireland and was kept a prisoner in Dublin and London until his death in 1585.

In 1570 Pope Pius V excommunicated Elizabeth I in the bull *Regnans in Excelsis*. From then on the popes were to look to military means to stop Elizabeth I. We will see how Pope Gregory XIII (1572-85) sent a small group of solders to assist Irish rebels against the queen.

From 1570 onwards conditions became much harder for Catholics in Ireland and especially for priests. In the eyes of Elizabeth I and her government, loyalty to the pope meant treason against the queen and support for her enemies abroad.

THE FIRST DESMOND REBELLION (1569-75)

We have seen that the two most powerful families in Munster were the Old English Fitzgeralds, earls of Desmond, and the Butler earls of Ormond. Because the Butlers of Ormond had been related to Elizabeth's mother, Ann Boleyn, and because they had become Protestants, the queen preferred them to the Catholic Fitzgeralds of Desmond.

In 1565 the earls of Desmond and Ormond fought each other at the Battle of Affane in Waterford. As a result Queen Elizabeth called both men to London and kept them there for a few years. While the earls were absent from Ireland, English adventurers tried to take over some of their lands in Munster. The most important of these were Sir Peter Carew and Sir Humphrey Gilbert. When the English government supported their claims, a rebellion broke out in Munster.

Gaelic chieftains like McCarthy Mór of Cork and Kerry joined with James Fitzmaurice Fitzgerald, a cousin of the earl of Desmond. As well as fearing the loss of their lands, the rebels also had religious grievances. They opposed the attempts of Elizabeth I to stamp out the Catholic religion in Ireland and appealed to the pope and to King Philip II of Spain for assistance. However, at that time Philip II wished to make peace with England so he refused to send help to the Irish rebels.

The rebellion in the Butler lands was easily defeated after the earl of Ormond persuaded his relations to make peace. The Fitzgeralds of Desmond now had no choice but to bring the war to an end in 1575.

Elizabeth I did not wish to prolong an expensive war in Munster. She therefore pardoned those involved in the First Desmond Rebellion. Even James Fitzmaurice Fitzgerald was forgiven. Soon afterwards he went abroad to Spain and Rome to seek help in planning another rebellion against Elizabeth.

TEST YOUR KNOWLEDGE
1 *Name the two main Old English families in Munster.*
2 *Which one did Elizabeth I prefer and why?*
3 *Name two English adventurers who claimed land in Munster during the 1560s.*
4 *What grievances, besides the loss of their lands, did the rebels have during the First Desmond Rebellion?*
5 *Why did Philip II fail to assist the Irish rebels?*
6 *How did Elizabeth I react to the ending of the First Desmond Rebellion?*
7 *What did its leader, James Fitzmaurice Fitzgerald, do after the rebellion ended?*

THE SECOND DESMOND REBELLION (1579-83)

In 1579 the Second Desmond Rebellion began in Munster when James Fitzmaurice Fitzgerald returned to Ireland with a small band of soldiers sent by Pope Gregory XIII (1572-85).

Fitzmaurice was a deeply religious man. At one time he had planned to enter a religious order in Europe but was persuaded to devote himself to fighting English rule in Ireland instead.

Fitzmaurice was determined to resist the spread of the Protestant rule of Elizabeth I by force of arms. However, after four years looking

Pope Gregory XIII talking to cardinals and other advisers.

for soldiers and money in Spain and Rome, all he managed to get was a small force of soldiers from the pope.

After an adventurous journey, Fitzmaurice and his small group of around 300 Italian and Spanish soldiers landed at Dingle, Co. Kerry, on 18 July 1579. As they came ashore hymns were chanted and a flag of the Holy Cross was planted in the ground.

Fitzmaurice called on the chieftains, lords and people of Ireland to support him in his war for the Catholic faith. Most local lords were afraid of English revenge if they supported the rebels. Even Fitzmaurice's own cousin, the earl of Desmond, hesitated to support him. When Fitzmaurice was killed in a skirmish soon afterwards, any hope of a united Irish resistance to Elizabeth I in Munster died with him.

THE MASSACRE AT SMERWICK (1580)

Soon after the death of James Fitzmaurice Fitzgerald, English officials forced the earl of Desmond into open rebellion against the queen. The earl hoped that he would receive troops from Spain and the pope. He called on all Irishmen 'to join in the defence of our Catholic faith against Englishmen who have overrun our country'.

The earl's call was answered in Leinster where Lord Baltinglass, an Old English lord, and the Gaelic chieftain, Fiach MacHugh O'Byrne, rose in rebellion. Despite O'Byrne's victory over the English, who were led by Lord Grey, at the Battle of Glenmalure in Co. Wicklow, the Leinster rebels were eventually defeated. O'Byrne surrendered to the English on favourable terms and Lord Baltinglass fled to Spain.

Meanwhile in Munster another expedition from the pope arrived to help the rebels. In September 1580 about 700 of the pope's soldiers landed at Smerwick, Co Kerry. About 200 were Spaniards and the rest were mainly Italians. They were under the command of Colonel San Joseph and they built defences around the fort at Smerwick called *Dún an Óir* in Irish.

An English army under Lord Deputy Grey arrived to besiege the fort. On 10 November 1580 the garrison was defeated by the English army and nearly all the defenders were massacred.

After their victory at Smerwick, the English forces marched through most of Munster, plundering and laying waste the territory of the earl of Desmond and other rebels. In November 1583 the last earl of Desmond was assassinated at Glenageenty near Tralee. His head was later sent to England and displayed in the Tower of London.

The last earl of Desmond is murdered near Tralee in 1583.

TEST YOUR KNOWLEDGE

1 How did the Second Desmond Rebellion begin in Ireland?
2 What was the main aim of James Fitzmaurice Fitzgerald?
3 Describe the landings of James Fitzmaurice Fitzgerald and his followers at Dingle in July 1579.
4 How did his death affect the rebellion?
5 What appeal did the earl of Desmond make when he joined the rebellion?
6 Name two Leinster lords who rebelled against the English in 1580.
7 Who won the Battle of Glenmalure (1580)?
8 Who landed at Smerwick, Co. Kerry, in September 1580?
9 What occurred after the English victory at Smerwick?
10 Who commanded the English forces there?
11 How did the earl of Desmond die in November 1583?
12 What treatment was meted out to the people and land of Munster by the English forces after the defeat of the Munster rebellion?

THE DESTRUCTION OF MUNSTER

With the complete defeat of the Desmond rebellion, the vast territories of the earl and his followers were taken over by Queen Elizabeth and preparations were made to plant them with loyal English settlers.

WORKING WITH EVIDENCE

The poet Edmund Spenser was in Ireland at the time of the rebellion in Munster. He has given us the following description of these events:

Notwithstanding that Munster was a most rich and powerful country, full of corn and cattle, before one year and a half, the people were brought to such wretchedness, as that any stony heart would have regretted.

Out of every corner of the woods and glens they came creeping forth upon their hands, for their legs could not bear them. They looked like anatomies of death, they spoke like ghosts crying out of their graves. They did eat of the dead bodies, the very carcasses they took out of their graves.

If they found a plot of watercress or shamrocks, there they flocked as to a feast for the time. . . . In a short space there were none almost left, and the most populous and beautiful country was suddenly made void of man and beast.

Edmund Spenser (1552-99).

1 *According to Spenser, what was the condition of Munster before the rebellion?*
2 *Describe the way the starving people moved.*
3 *How does Spenser describe their appearance?*
4 *Give two examples of behaviour which show the extreme hunger of the people.*
5 *Do you think that Spenser had sympathy for the people of Munster? Explain your answer.*

THE PLANTATION OF MUNSTER

The rebellion in Munster gave the land-hungry English adventurers the opportunity they had been waiting for. The province lay burnt and devastated. Disease and famine were widespread, killing many who escaped death in the wars.

The English government now drew up new maps of the area in preparation for a plantation. Over half a million acres of land were taken from the earl of Desmond alone. This was scattered throughout Cork, Kerry, Limerick and Waterford.

In 1586 Queen Elizabeth and her advisers approved a plan worked out for the plantation of Munster. The following rules are from the *Scheme of Plantation* accepted by the queen on 21 June 1586.

WORKING WITH EVIDENCE

- *Her majesty* doth assent that all lands come into her hands in the province of Munster shall be divided into estates of 12,000, 8,000, 6,000 and 4,000 acres.
- None shall undertake for himself a greater portion than 12,000 acres.
- None of the English people to be there planted shall make over any estate to the 'mere' Irish.
- No 'mere' Irish shall be permitted in any family there.
- For the next seven years, they shall be defended by garrisons at the queen's charge.

What was the largest type of estate under Munster plantation?
Why do you think planters were not allowed to gain estates larger than this?
Were the planters allowed to grant lands to the 'mere' Irish? Why do you think this was so?
Why do you think marriage with 'mere' Irish was forbidden to the planters?
What protection did the queen offer the settlers in the early years of the plantation?

Although the upper limit of 12,000 acres was set on the size of estates under the Munster plantation, Sir Walter Raleigh, a favourite of Queen Elizabeth, received an estate of 42,000 acres near Youghal, Co. Cork.

These estates were to be rented out to English settlers known as *undertakers*. They got this name because they undertook or agreed to bring over English customs and the Protestant religion and, above all, to remain loyal to the queen. Many of the undertakers were the younger sons of lords from the western parts of England.

The undertakers were also expected to introduce English methods of farming to Munster and to avoid taking on the native Irish as tenants. The English government hoped that Munster would be loyal to the queen and safe from the threat of Spanish invasion in the future.

Walter Raleigh [1]52-1618) was [on]e of the first [peo]ple to bring [tob]acco from [Am]erica to [Eu]rope. In the [pla]ntation of [Mu]nster, Raleigh [wa]s given vast [est]ates near [Yo]ughal in Co. [Cor]k.

The Munster plantation.

Planted areas

HOW THE PLANTATION WORKED

The plantation of Munster did not work out as well as the English government had hoped. Much of the land had been so badly damaged during the wars that it was difficult to farm it. There was also the constant danger of attack from the Irish who had been driven off their land. As a result, many planters returned to England in disappointment and only about 3,000 English settlers decided to remain. Because so few remained, they had to employ native Irish servants and labourers and to rent out land to them. This made the plantation insecure and likely to suffer from attack in the event of a future rebellion.

Despite these setbacks, those who chose to remain enjoyed some prosperity for a while. They rebuilt ruined castles and houses, introduced new farming methods and became rich by exporting timber. By 1597 land which had fetched sixpence an acre ten years before was now being let at five times that amount.

The planters also built up plantation towns such as Bandon, Killarney and Tallow. These became centres for trade and the administration of law in the local area. By 1600, however, the new plantation was almost in ruin.

TEST YOUR KNOWLEDGE
1 *Describe the condition of Munster after the Desmond rebellion.*
2 *How much land belonging to the earl of Desmond was to be planted with new English settlers?*
3 *How was the land divided?*
4 *Who were the undertakers?*
5 *Write down two reasons why the plantation of Munster did not work out as well as expected.*
6 *Why were many native Irish servants and labourers employed by the settlers?*
7 *Name three plantation towns.*

THE PLANTATION UNDER ATTACK

In their eagerness to build houses and develop their farms, the planters had neglected to provide enough soldiers to defend the plantation. In 1598, when Hugh O'Neill sent an army to Munster under Owney O'More, many of the native Irish and Old English joined in to attack the planters. Those who could not escape to England fled to walled towns such as Youghal, Cork or Limerick where they prepared to set sail for England. Those who failed to escape were killed and their castles or houses and crops were burned.

One planter who managed to escape was the English poet, Edmund Spenser. He had an estate at Kilcolman near Fermoy in Co. Cork, and here he wrote part of his famous poem, *The Faerie Queen.*

A planter family flee in terror from attack by the Gaelic Irish.

Spenser and his family barely managed to escape and reach the safety of the walls of Cork.

After the defeat of the Irish at the Battle of Kinsale in 1601 the plantation began again. Some of the old settlers returned, but many more remained in England. Their land was taken over by adventurers such as Richard Boyle, earl of Cork.

The English government was to learn some valuable lessons from the plantation in Munster. The next major plantation took place in Ulster during the reign of Elizabeth's successor, James I (1603-25).

We will see in chapter 10 that much greater care was taken to ensure that the new plantation would be a success.

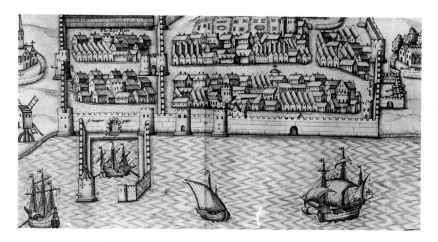

Many planters fled to the safety of walled towns such as Youghal when they were attacked by the Gaelic Irish in 1598.

Chapter 8: Review

- Elizabeth I, like the other Tudor rulers before her, was determined to strengthen English rule in Ireland. She feared that her foreign enemies might attack England through Ireland. As a result she borrowed huge sums of money to conquer the country.

- As soon as Elizabeth became queen she set about restoring the Protestant religion in Ireland. In 1560 the Irish parliament passed two acts: the Act of Supremacy, making her supreme governor of the Church of Ireland, and the Act of Uniformity, which laid down that everybody should attend Sunday service in the local Protestant church.

- All Irish people had to pay taxes called tithes to the Protestant Church of Ireland, which now became the State or official Church. All services in the Church were according to the Book of Common Prayer. However, little progress was made in spreading the Protestant religion throughout Ireland.

- With the arrival of the Counter-Reformation, the Catholic Church began organising a revival in Ireland. In 1560 the pope sent a Jesuit priest named David Woulfe to travel around Ireland collect information on the condition of Catholics.

- By the end of Elizabeth's reign the Catholic Counter-Reformation had beer successful in Ireland and the Catholic religion remained the faith of most people.

- The two most powerful families in Munster were the Fitzgeralds of Desmor and the Butlers of Ormond. Elizabeth preferred the Butlers as they were Protestants and related to her mother. However, in 1564 when the earl of Ormond and the earl of Desmond fough they were both summoned to England. I their absence English adventurers tried to take over their lands. This led to a rebellion in Munster led by McCarthy Mór and James Fitzmaurice Fitzgerald, a cousin of the earl of Desmond.

- The First Desmond Rebellion ended in 1575 when Elizabeth pardoned all those involved. However, James Fitzmaurice went to Spain and Rome to seek help to start another rebellion against England.

- In 1579 the Second Desmond Rebellion began when James Fitzmaurice Fitzgeral eturned to Ireland with a small band of soldiers sent by the pope. He was a deeply religious man and wanted to start a religious war against Protestant England. When he landed at Dingle he received little local support and was killed in a skirmish soon afterwards.

The earl of Desmond was now forced into open rebellion against the queen. He received support in Leinster from Lord Baltinglass and Fiach MacHugh O'Byrne, but the Leinster rebels were soon defeated.

A new force of about 700 soldiers was sent by the pope and arrived at Smerwick harbour where they built a fort (Dún an Óir). However, an English army defeated them and all were massacred. In 1583 the earl of Desmond was himself murdered. The Second Desmond Rebellion had been ruthlessly put down and the vast territories of Munster lay in the hands of the English.

The plantation of Munster began in 1586 when all the confiscated lands were divided into large estates to be rented to English planters.

- The planters were forbidden to rent their estates to the native Irish or to marry among them.

- Sir Walter Raleigh, a favourite of Queen Elizabeth, was given a vast estate near Youghal in Co. Cork. The poet Edmund Spenser received an estate near Fermoy in the same county.

- The plantation faced a number of difficulties: the settlers were constantly attacked; many native Irish tenants and servants were employed; and the estates were too large.

- However, the planters introduced new farming methods to Munster as well as building castles and setting up new towns.

- The settlers neglected to defend themselves properly and the plantation was destroyed by the native Irish during a rebellion in 1598. But after the defeat of the Irish at the Battle of Kinsale in 1601 the plantation of Munster was restored.

ACTIVITIES

1 Complete the following sentences:
  (a) The Protestant Church established by Queen Elizabeth was known as _____.
  (b) In 1570 Pope Pius V excommunicated _____.
  (c) In 1579 James Fitzmaurice Fitzgerald landed at _____.
  (d) In November 1583 the earl of Desmond was _____.
  (e) An adventurer was _____.

2 Multiple choice
  (a) Queen Elizabeth I gained vast areas of land in Munster when: (i) the Kildares were defeated; (ii) she was given the land by the Desmond family; (iii) the Desmond rebellion was put down; (iv) the O'Moores and the O'Connors were defeated.
  (b) A vivid description of the destruction of Munster was given by: (i) Edmund Spenser; (ii) Richard Boyle; (iii) Sir Walter Raleigh; (iv) the earl of Desmond.
  (c) The planters in Munster came under attack because: (i) they did not build enough houses; (ii) they neglected to provide enough soldiers to defend themselves; (iii) they farmed the land badly; (iv) they attacked the native Irish.

3 *Fill in the blanks using the words in the box.*

Edmund Spenser	**the Desmond Rebellion**
Queen Elizabeth I	**the Gaelic Irish**
Walter Raleigh	**undertakers**
English settlers	

With the complete defeat of _____, the vast territories of the earl were take over by _____. Plans were then made to plant these lands with _____. Under the rules of the plantation, planters known as _____ agreed to practise English customs and the Protestant religion in Munster. A huge estate near Youghal was given to _____. A famous English poet, _____, had a vast estate near Fermoy in Co. Cork. The plantation was under constant attack from _____.

4 *Write about the Munster plantation under the following headings:*
   (a) How the land was divided.
   (b) The settlers.
   (c) The reason why the plantation failed.

5 *Write a paragraph on the religious policy of Queen Elizabeth I in Ireland.*

THE NINE YEARS WAR

THE GAELIC CHIEFTAINS OF ULSTER

In Munster the most powerful landowners were the Old English lords, the earl of Ormond and the earl of Desmond. In Ulster, however, most of the land was under the rule of Gaelic chieftains. The two most powerful of these were the leader of the O'Neills in Tyrone and the head of the O'Donnells in Donegal.

Up to 1600 most of Ulster was still outside the control of the English government. In this part of Ireland the ancient Gaelic way of life still remained largely undisturbed. There were few towns, and farming was carried out in the Gaelic manner. Catholic priests enjoyed the protection of the local chieftains.

As early as 1560, however, Queen Elizabeth had experienced her first rebellion in Ulster. The ruler responsible was a member of the O'Neill family: *Shane the Proud.*

SHANE THE PROUD

Shane was the son of Con Baccah O'Neill and had become chieftain under the old Gaelic Brehon law. Under English law his elder brother, Matthew, should have been chieftain, but Elizabeth I was willing to let Shane remain as chieftain if he kept the peace. She wanted to avoid a costly war in Ireland.

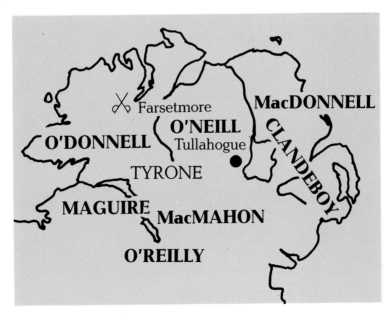

The main clans of Ulster at the time of Shane the Proud. Note Tullahogue, the location of the inaugural stone of the O'Neills.

Shane had no intention of remaining at peace with his neighbours. He was a proud and vain man and his desire to extend his rule over all of Ulster earned him the nickname 'Shane the Proud'.

Shane employed over 1,500 Scots mercenary troops, known as Redshanks because of their deerskin leggings. He also armed all of the men of his clan, not just the freemen as was the tradition in Ireland. In 1561 he attacked and defeated the O'Donnells of Tyrconnell who were loyal to Elizabeth at that time. The queen sent her lord deputy, the earl of Sussex, to attack Shane.

Shane's forces kept escaping into the woods and bogs, and Sussex found it impossible to defeat them. After seeing the strong army which Sussex had gathered together, Shane decided that it would be wiser for him to go to London to plead his case with the queen.

WORKING WITH EVIDENCE

Read this passage and answer the questions which follow.

Shane O'Neill visits the court of Queen Elizabeth

In 1562 Shane O'Neill came to London to the court of Her Majesty Queen Elizabeth. With him came a group of followers dressed and armed in the Irish manner. They were bare-headed with long, flowing curls and wore bright yellow shirts with large sleeves, along with large cloaks made from rough material. They were armed with huge battle axes.

The queen received O'Neill with great courtesy and he knelt before her and asked pardon for waging wars against his neighbours and against the English forces in Ireland. Her Majesty then asked him why he had refused to allow Hugh, his brother Matthew's son, to occupy his lands. Shane replied that under Irish custom and Brehon law he had been proclaimed chieftain of the O'Neills.

In all, O'Neill remained in London for six months. He refused to attend Protestant services but instead went to mass at the Spanish embassy. It is quite possible that he went there to plot with the Spaniards against Her Majesty. Before his return to Ireland, O'Neill promised to end his attacks on his neighbours and to live as a faithful subject of her majesty.

(Adapted from a contemporary account)

1 *Who accompanied Shane O'Neill on his visit to London in 1562?*
2 *Describe the dress of Shane's followers.*
3 *How were they armed?*
4 *How did Queen Elizabeth receive O'Neill?*
5 *Why did the queen ask him about the rights of Hugh, his brother Matthew's son?*
6 *What was Shane's reply?*
7 *How did O'Neill show his attitude to Elizabeth's religion?*
8 *What promise did he make to the queen before returning to Ireland?*

THE BATTLE OF FARSETMORE (1567) AND THE DEATH OF SHANE THE PROUD

On his return from England, Shane was at the height of his power. He defeated the McDonnells of Antrim at Glenshesk in 1565 with the queen's approval. Elizabeth had allowed him to attack the McDonnells because they were loyal to Scotland, which was an enemy of England at that time. Shane, however, soon broke his word to the queen and attacked other clans as well. He forced the Maguires of Fermanagh and the O'Reillys of Cavan to submit to him and was well on the way to placing all of Ulster under his control.

In 1567 Sir Henry Sidney, the lord deputy, marched into Ulster and captured most of Shane's treasure from an island in Lough Neagh. Shane then attacked the O'Donnells of Tyrconnell who were loyal to the English. The O'Donnells, assisted by a large force of gallowglasses, defeated Shane O'Neill at the Battle of Farsetmore in Donegal.

Shane now had a choice – to trust the English or to seek refuge with his old enemies, the McDonnells of Antrim. He foolishly fled to Antrim, and the McDonnells murdered him during a quarrel at Cushendun in 1567. They cut off his head and sent it to the lord deputy as proof of their loyalty to Queen Elizabeth. The head of Shane the Proud was placed on a spike outside Dublin Castle as a warning to all who rebelled against the queen.

Although he had looked in vain to the Catholic rulers of France and Spain for help against Elizabeth, Shane was not really interested in religion. He was a cruel and ruthless man, anxious for allies in his fight to make himself ruler of all Ulster. With his death Elizabeth I and her government in Ireland had lost one of their most dangerous enemies.

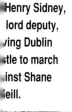

Henry Sidney, lord deputy, ⌐ing Dublin ⌐tle to march ⌐inst Shane ⌐eill.

Shane O'Neill is stabbed to death by the McDonnells of Antrim in 1567.

TEST YOUR KNOWLEDGE

TEST YOUR KNOWLEDGE

1   *What clan did Shane O'Neill defeat at the Battle of Glenshesk in 1565?*
2   *Why did Elizabeth I support Shane's defeat of his clan?*
3   *Name two Ulster clans which Shane forced into submission.*
4   *What successful move was made by the lord deputy, Sir Henry Sidney, against Shane O'Neill in 1567?*
5   *Which Ulster clan defeated Shane the Proud at the Battle of Farsetmore in 1567?*
6   *Name the clan which murdered Shane.*
7   *Why was Shane O'Neill's head placed on a spike at Dublin Castle?*

HUGH O'NEILL (1550-1616)

After the murder of Shane the Proud in 1567, Turlough became the new chieftain of the O'Neill clan. For a time Ulster seemed peaceful. Hugh O'Neill, the young son of Matthew, was brought to England and reared as a Protestant in the home of Sir Philip Sidney and in the queen's court. Elizabeth intended to use him, when the time was right, to spread English influence in Ulster.

Hugh O'Neill returned to Ireland as the baron of Dungannon and to all appearances seemed to be a loyal Englishman. He even helped the queen's forces to put down the Desmond rebellion in Munster. Because of his loyalty he was made earl of Tyrone in 1585. But by the time he became chieftain of the clan in 1593, Hugh O'Neill had come to see himself as a Gaelic ruler rather than an English lord. He hated the interference of English officials in his lands and realised that the Gaelic way of life could only be preserved by getting rid of all English influence.

Acting very cautiously, Hugh O'Neill prepared for a war which would decide the future of Gaelic Ireland.

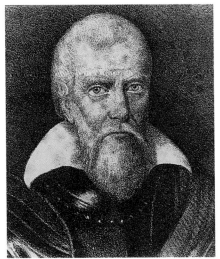

Hugh O'Neill.

The castle of Hugh O'Neill at Dungannon, Co. Tyrone.

TEST YOUR KNOWLEDGE
1   Who became chieftain of the O'Neill clan after the death of Shane?
2   Who was the father of Hugh O'Neill?
3   Where was Hugh O'Neill educated?
4   Why do you think he was brought to England?
5   How did Hugh O'Neill prove his loyalty to the queen? What title did she give him?
6   When did he become chieftain of the O'Neill clan?
7   'Hugh O'Neill had come to see himself as a Gaelic ruler rather than an English lord.' Explain what is meant by this.

PREPARATIONS FOR A WAR

While Hugh O'Neill still appeared to be loyal to England, he began secretly to prepare for a war.

- He built up supplies of weapons and ammunition and trained his men in their use. He was only allowed a small regular army so he recruited men, trained them, dismissed them and recruited more. As a result, Hugh soon had at his service in Ulster a large army of well-trained men. He ordered a huge quantity of lead which he said was needed to repair the roof of his castle in Dungannon. In fact the lead was to be used to make bullets.
- Hugh O'Neill realised that a war against England could not succeed without foreign help. He wrote to King Philip II of Spain asking for help in a Catholic war against Protestant England. He hoped that Philip would welcome the chance of avenging the defeat of the Spanish Armada in 1588.
- In addition to foreign aid, Hugh O'Neill built up friendships or alliances with the other clans of Ulster. He did this by marriage alliances. His greatest friend was Red Hugh O'Donnell.

RED HUGH O'DONNELL (1572-1602)

Relations between the O'Neills and their neighbours, the O'Donnells of Tyrconnell, had been very bad since the time of Shane the Proud. However, this was soon to change.

When The O'Donnell refused to allow an English sheriff into Tyrconnell, lord deputy Perrot ordered the kidnapping of the chieftain's fifteen-year-old son, Red Hugh, in 1587. The young boy, with two companions, was kept in Dublin Castle as a hostage to ensure the loyalty of his father. After making several attempts to escape, the boys eventually succeeded on Christmas Eve 1591. In an effort to reach Fiach MacHugh O'Byrne, the boys made their way across the Wicklow Mountains in the freezing snow of winter. By the time they were found by O'Byrne, one of the boys – Art O'Neill – had died from frostbite and

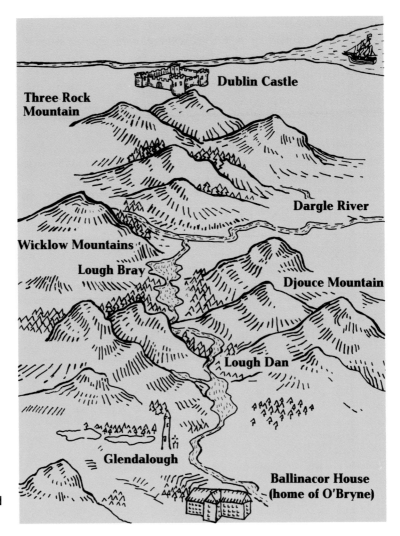

Three Rock Mountain

Dublin Castle

Dargle River

Wicklow Mountains

Lough Bray

Djouce Mountain

Lough Dan

Glendalough

Ballinacor House
(home of O'Bryne)

The escape of Red
Hugh O'Donnell and
Art O'Neill (1591).

starvation. Red Hugh recovered in the home of the O'Byrnes but as a result of his experiences he was to walk with limp for the rest of his life.

Red Hugh then made his way home to Ulster, where he received a great welcome from Hugh O'Neill in Dungannon Castle. When his father died, Red Hugh became chieftain of the O'Donnell clan and was to be one of Hugh O'Neill's greatest and most loyal allies. His imprisonment in Dublin Castle led him to hate English rule. Like O'Neill, he was prepared to go to war to preserve the Gaelic way of life. The alliance between the two families became even more secure when Red Hugh married a daughter of Hugh O'Neill.

TEST YOUR KNOWLEDGE
1   *How did Hugh O'Neill start building up his army?*
2   *Why did he order a large quantity of lead?*
3   *To what foreign ruler did he write for help?*
4   *Who became Hugh O'Neill's greatest ally in Ulster?*

5 *Why was Red Hugh O'Donnell kidnapped in 1587?*
6 *When did the boys escape from the castle and where did they go?*
7 *How was Red Hugh affected by his imprisonment?*
8 *Who welcomed Red Hugh on his return to Ulster?*

FIGHTING BREAKS OUT: THE BEGINNING OF THE NINE YEARS WAR

War broke out in 1593, a bit sooner than Hugh O'Neill would have liked. McMahon of Monaghan and Maguire of Fermanagh – both allies of O'Neill – quarrelled with the government and attacked a garrison at Enniskillen. They were helped by O'Donnell who was anxious for war. Hugh O'Neill was not yet ready to rebel openly against the English, but he secretly helped his Gaelic allies.

The forces of the lord deputy were defeated in a battle which has since become known as the Battle of the Ford of the Biscuits, so called because when the English fled they left their food supplies behind them. This battle was the beginning of a war between the Gaelic chieftains of Ulster and the English forces which was to last for nine years.

By 1595 Hugh O'Neill believed that the time was right to start an open rebellion against the queen. He called on all Catholics to join in a religious war against Protestant England. He defeated the lord deputy's forces at Clontibret in Co. Monaghan in 1595. Rebellion soon spread throughout the country. O'Donnell successfully invaded Connaught, while in Leinster O'Byrne rose up against the lord deputy. In Munster O'Neill was supported by many Old English who drove out some of the settlers who had come over during the plantation.

England's lord deputy sent army after army to attack Ulster, but they all failed to penetrate the province since it was cut off from the rest of

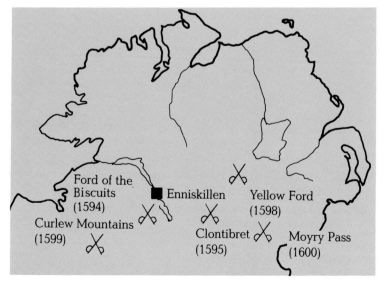

Ford of the Biscuits (1594)
Curlew Mountains (1599)
Enniskillen
Clontibret (1595)
Yellow Ford (1598)
Moyry Pass (1600)

main battles of the Nine Years War

Ulster during the Nine Years War.

the country by mountain, forest and bog. There seemed to be no stopping the combined forces of Ulster who were to experience their greatest victory in 1598 at the Battle of the Yellow Ford.

THE BATTLE OF THE YELLOW FORD

On 12 August 1598 an English force under the command of Marshall Bagenal marched against O'Neill. Bagenal had a personal hatred for Hugh O'Neill as he had earlier eloped with the marshall's nineteen-year-old sister, Mabel. The Irish forces made their stand just outside Armagh at a crossing point on the river Blackwater known as the Yellow Ford. O'Neill ordered his men to dig a two-metre-deep trench about two kilometres in length. They also dug pits in front of the trench and covered them with brush so that the movement of the enemy cavalry would be hampered. Although the English and Irish forces were nearly equal in number, Bagenal's army had far superior weapons. However, O'Neill's defensive tactics paid off. Each English regiment failed to penetrate the Irish defences and many soldiers, including Bagenal himself, were killed.

When the battle ended, English losses amounted to 1,500, while the Irish had lost around 400 men. The Battle of the Yellow Ford was to be the greatest Gaelic victory of the Nine Years War. As a result, English influence was almost confined to the walled towns. Elizabeth now realised that urgent and drastic action would be needed if she wanted to preserve English rule in Ireland.

TEST YOUR KNOWLEDGE
1 *Who had quarrelled with the English government in 1593? What was O'Neill's reaction to it?*
2 *What was the first Irish victory in the Nine Years War?*
3 *Where did Hugh O'Neill defeat the lord deputy's forces in 1595?*
4 *What support did O'Neill get in other parts of Ireland?*
5 *Who led the English forces in the Battle of the Yellow Ford?*
6 *Where did this battle take place? What orders did O'Neill give to his men?*
7 *What was the outcome of the battle and why was it so important?*

LORD MOUNTJOY ARRIVES IN IRELAND

In 1599 the queen sent Robert Devereaux, second earl of Essex, to Ireland in charge of a huge army of 20,000 men. Instead of marching against Ulster, Essex attacked Munster and was defeated at the Pass of the Plumes. Elizabeth was more furious than ever when he made a truce with O'Neill, while O'Donnell extended his control of Connaught, winning a major victory over English forces at the Curlew Hills. Elizabeth called Essex back to England and replaced him with a general who was to prove both brilliant and ruthless. This man was Lord Mountjoy.

ish soldiers
he march
nst Ulster
ng the Nine
rs War.

Lord Mountjoy.

Mountjoy first arrived in Ireland in 1600 at a time when English influence was again almost confined to the Pale. He believed that new methods were needed if the Gaelic chieftains of Ulster were to be defeated. He used ships to build a number of forts along the coast of Ulster beyond the Irish lines. One such fort at Derry was manned by 4,000 men. From these strongholds, the English attacked the Gaelic Irish, destroying their homes, burning their crops and stealing their cattle. In this way Mountjoy hoped to frighten and starve O'Neill's allies into submission. Mountjoy used the same ruthless methods to put down rebellion in Leinster and Munster.

The English troops forced the retreat of the Irish forces at the Moyry Pass. Hugh O'Neill was now desperate for the news of the promised help from Spain.

Ireland during the Nine Years War, showing O'Neill's march to Kinsale.

SPANISH HELP ARRIVES

Philip II had first sent a huge fleet to Ireland in 1596 and again in the following year, but both were forced back to Spain by violent storms. In September 1601 a Spanish fleet of about 3,500 men eventually arrived in Ireland. Instead of landing in the north, the fleet, under the command of Don Juan del Aguila, arrived in Kinsale, Co. Cork. An English army commanded by Mountjoy immediately marched southwards, pursued by O'Neill and O'Donnell. All arrived around the same time at the beginning of December 1601. The scene was now set for one of the most decisive battles in Irish history.

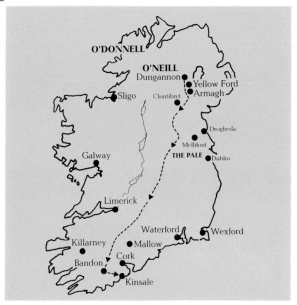

A view of the Battle of Kinsale (1601) showing the Spanish fleet at anchor in the bay.

THE BATTLE OF KINSALE

At Kinsale the Spanish fleet was surrounded by the English forces. When O'Neill and O'Donnell arrived they in turn surrounded the English. It now seemed as if Mountjoy's forces were trapped. O'Neill wanted to wait patiently until the English were starved into submission. The Spanish commander, del Aguila, and Red Hugh O'Donnell were both urging a quick attack. O'Neill eventually gave in and agreed to attack the English at dawn on Christmas Eve 1601. Mountjoy had learned of their plans and was ready for them. Within hours the Irish had lost the battle. The Irish troops had fled and the Spanish attack came too late. Del Aguila agreed peace terms with the English while O'Donnell fled to Spain and Hugh O'Neill returned to Ulster.

The Battle of Kinsale not only marked the end of the Nine Years War. It also brought about the final destruction of the power of the Gaelic chieftains.

TEST YOUR KNOWLEDGE
1 *Whom did the queen send to Ireland in 1599?*
2 *Why was she displeased with Essex?*
3 *Who came to Ireland in 1600 as lord deputy?*
4 *Describe how Mountjoy dealt with the Gaelic chieftains.*
5 *Where did the Spanish fleet arrive in 1601? Who commanded this fleet?*
6 *Why did Mountjoy's forces seem trapped at Kinsale?*
7 *What did O'Neill want to do at Kinsale?*
8 *What was the outcome of the Battle of Kinsale? Why was it so important?*

THE TREATY OF MELLIFONT (1603)

After his victory at Kinsale, Mountjoy marched northwards to Ulster. He burned the crops and forced O'Neill's remaining supporters to surrender. He captured the O'Neill stronghold at Dungannon and made it into an English fort. The ancient stone of Tullahogue, where for hundreds of years the rulers of the O'Neills had been proclaimed as chieftains, was destroyed for ever. Hugh O'Neill himself was forced to retreat into the woods to escape the plundering of Mountjoy and his forces. Eventually he decided to surrender to Mountjoy.

Hugh O'Neill met the lord deputy at Mellifont and signed the *Treaty of Mellifont* in March 1603. While O'Neill was allowed to hold on to his lands, he had to promise to give up Gaelic customs, live according to English law, and allow English officials such as sheriffs into his territory.

WORKING WITH EVIDENCE

The following is an account of O'Neill's surrender at Mellifont. Read it and answer the questions which follow.

O'Neill surrenders at Mellifont
The lord deputy, Mountjoy, was at Mellifont when he received news of the death of Elizabeth (24 March 1603). He decided not to let O'Neill know of this until after the treaty was signed.

On 30 March Hugh O'Neill, earl of Tyrone, and his followers came to Mellifont in the afternoon. On being admitted to the lord deputy's presence, the earl of Tyrone knelt at the door for a long space of time, making humble submission to Her Majesty the Queen. After being required to come nearer to the lord deputy, he performed the same ceremony for about the space of one hour.

On the next day O'Neill made a humble submission in writing which he presented while kneeling to the lord deputy and council and in the presence of a great assembly of people.

On the next day an English ship arrived at Dublin with letters from the lords of England advertising the queen's death and proclaiming James I king of England, Scotland and Ireland. The earl of Tyrone on hearing of the queen's death could not stop himself from shedding tears. Although O'Neill claimed that he was sorry for the loss of the queen, this proud man might never have signed the treaty if he had known of Elizabeth's death.

(Adapted from an account written by an Englishman named Fynes Moryson who was present at Mellifont)

1 *Why do you think Mountjoy decided not to tell O'Neill of Elizabeth's death?*
2 *When did Hugh O'Neill and his followers come to Mellifont?*
3 *Describe what O'Neill did when he met the lord deputy.*
4 *How did O'Neill react to the news of the queen's death?*
5 *Read the last sentence in the extract carefully. What do you think it means?*

Hugh O'Neill surrendering to Mountjoy at Mellifont in 16...

Chapter 9: Review

- In the early years of Elizabeth's reign she faced a war in Ulster against Shane O'Neill. He wanted to extend his rule over all of Ulster and as a result went to war with his neighbours, the O'Donnells of Tyrconnell.

- The queen sent her lord deputy, the earl of Sussex, to attack Shane but he proved impossible to defeat. He decided to go to London to plead his case with the queen. In 1562 he arrived at the queen's court with a group of armed gallowglasses and Irish wolfhounds. He promised the queen to end his attacks on his neighbours and to keep the peace.

- On his return to Ireland, Shane immediately broke his promise to the queen. While his attack on the McDonnells of Antrim was approved by the queen, he also attacked other clans in Ulster. The O'Donnells of Tyrconnell defeated Shane at the Battle of Farsetmore. He now turned to his old enemies, the McDonnells, for help, but the McDonnells murdered him in 1567.

- Hugh O'Neill, the son of Matthew, was brought to England as a young boy and reared as a Protestant in the home of Sir Philip Sidney and in the queen's court. It was hoped that he would be loyal to England and help spread English influence in Ulster. However, by the time Hugh O'Neill, earl of Tyrone, was elected chieftain of the O'Neill clan in 1593, he was determined to rid Ulster of all English influence.

- He made preparations for a war against England by building up supplies of weapons and recruiting and training soldiers. He also wrote to Philip II of Spain asking for help in a religious war against Protestant England.

- Hugh O'Neill also became friends or allies with the other Gaelic chieftains in Ulster. His greatest ally was Red Hugh O'Donnell. As a boy Red Hugh had been kidnapped by the English and imprisoned in Dublin Castle. As a result he hated English rule and, like O'Neill, was prepared to go to war to preserve the old Gaelic way of life.

- The Nine Years War began in 1593 when O'Neill's allies, the McMahons and the Maguires, attacked an English garrison at Enniskillen. O'Donnell joined them and they defeated the English at the Battle of the Ford of the Biscuits.

By 1595 O'Neill declared open warfare against England and defeated the lord deputy's forces at Clontibret. Rebellion spread to the rest of the country when O'Donnell invaded Connaught, O'Byrne rose in Leinster, and Old English allies of O'Neill drove some settlers from their lands in Munster.

The greatest victory for the Gaelic chieftains came in August 1598 when O'Neill's army defeated an English army, led by Marshall Bagenal, at the Battle of the Yellow Ford just outside Armagh.

In 1599 the queen sent the earl of Essex to Ireland in charge of a huge army. Essex failed to attack O'Neill so the queen replaced him in 1600 with a brilliant and ruthless general named Lord Mountjoy. Mountjoy built forts along the coast of Ulster and forced O'Neill's allies to surrender by burning their crops and stealing their cattle.

- In September 1601 a Spanish fleet of 3,500 men arrived in Kinsale, Co. Cork, under the command of Don Juan del Aguila. Mountjoy's forces surrounded the Spanish, while O'Donnell and O'Neill surrounded the English. The Irish made the fateful decision to attack and were defeated on Christmas Day 1601.

- Mountjoy moved northwards and overran O'Neill territory. O'Neill eventually surrendered in March 1603 at Mellifont, where he promised to rule according to English laws and to allow English sheriffs into his territory.

ACTIVITIES

Complete the following sentences:
(a) The two main Gaelic rulers in Ulster around 1590 were _____ .
(b) The Battle of the Yellow Ford (1598) was won by _____ .
(c) The leader of the English forces at the Battle of Kinsale was _____ .
(d) The treaty which ended the Nine Years War was _____ .
(e) Under the terms of this treaty Hugh O'Neill was _____ .

Match an item in column 1 with an item in column 2.

COLUMN 1	COLUMN 2
Queen Elizabeth's lord deputy	Hugh O'Neill
Leader of Spanish forces at Kinsale	Shane the Proud
Battle of the Yellow Ford	Red Hugh O'Donnell
Gaelic ruler from Donegal	Lord Mountjoy
The Battle of Farsetmore	Don Juan del Aguila

Give an account of the Battle of Kinsale (1601) from the point of view of an English soldier.

Write a paragraph on the Treaty of Mellifont.

THE PLANTATION OF ULSTER

After the Treaty of Mellifont, some of the English officials were very annoyed that O'Neill and the other Ulster chieftains had been allowed to keep their lands. They had hoped that the government would take over these territories and divide them among English settlers, including themselves.

The new lord deputy, Sir Arthur Chichester, travelled around Ulster enforcing English laws and customs. By 1607 O'Neill and the other Gaelic chieftains could no longer put up with the restrictions on their power. They decided to leave Ireland for ever.

THE FLIGHT OF THE EARLS

In September 1607 Hugh O'Neill, earl of Tyrone and Rory O'Donnell, earl of Tyrconnell, set sail from Lough Swilly for the continent of Europe. They were accompanied by around a hundred followers from the leading Gaelic families. O'Neill had been called to London and, knowing that he risked possible execution, he and his followers decided on sudden flight from Ireland. This event has become known as *The Flight of the Earls*. The Irish people in Ulster were now leaderless and the province was completely in the control of the English government.

O'Neill and the other chieftains failed to get the king of Spain and the pope to intervene in Ireland once again. By the time of his death in Rome in 1616 the once-powerful Hugh O'Neill was worn out by blindness, disease and disappointment. Back in Ireland Sir Arthur

The Flight of the Earls.

Chichester and other English officials were delighted when the Flight of the Earls took place. Now at last they could take control of vast parts of Ulster and hand over land to English and Scottish settlers who would practise the Protestant religion and remain loyal to the king.

WORKING WITH EVIDENCE

These two accounts date from around the time of the Flight of the Earls. Account A is by Sir John Davies, an English official, while Account B was written by an Irish Franciscan.

Account A

It is true that they have set sail, men, women and children on 14 September. It is certain that the earl of Tyrone (Hugh O'Neill) in his heart sorrows at the English government in his country, where until his last submission, as well before his rebellion as in the time of his rebellion, he ever lived like a free prince, or rather like an absolute tyrant there. But now the law of England and the officials enforcing it were like shackles and handlocks to him; the garrisons planted in his country were like thorns in his side. . . .

The English here are glad to see the day when law and government have banished Tyrone out of Ireland, which the best army in Europe and the expense of two millions of sterling pounds did not bring to pass.

Account B

A ship put in at the harbour of Swilly and in it there departed from Ireland the earl O'Neill, the earl O'Donnell with a great number of the chieftains of the province of Ulster. They entered the ship on the Festival of the Holy Cross in autumn (14 September).

This was a distinguished crew for one ship. It is certain that the sea had not supported or the winds had not wafted from Ireland, in modern times, a party more famous for valour, prowess or high achievement. . . . Woe to the mind that thought up the project of their setting out on this voyage, without knowing whether they should ever return to their native land from the end of the world.

Both writers have strong feelings on the topic they describe. Give an example from each extract which shows these feelings.

How did Sir John Davies (Account A) describe O'Neill's status as a ruler up to a short time before the Flight of the Earls?

Is this a biased description? Explain your answer.

What images are used in Account A to describe the effects of English law on O'Neill's freedom?

What was the reaction of the English officials to the departure of O'Neill?

On what, do you think, did the English government have to spend 'two millions of sterling pounds'?

Would you agree that the author of Account B shows his sympathy for the earls from an early stage? Support your answer by referring to the account.

What tribute does the author of Account B pay to the bravery of the departing earls?

The account ends with a curse. Who is cursed and why?

It is clear from both accounts that an event of great importance is being described. Would you agree with this? Support your answer.

THE PLANTATION OF ULSTER

After the Flight of the Earls, six of the nine counties of Ulster were taken over directly by King James I. These counties – Donegal, Derry, Fermanagh, Tyrone, Armagh and Cavan – were to be part of a vast plantation under English and Scottish settlers. Three Ulster counties were not included in this plantation: Monaghan, Antrim and Down.

Co. Monaghan had been taken over by Elizabeth I in 1591 and handed back to its former rulers, the MacMahons and MacKennas, provided they remained loyal to England. Counties Antrim and Down had already been settled by colonists from Scotland.

King James I (1603-25) became king of England on the death of Elizabeth I in 1603. Under his rule, the Ulster plantation took place.

In 1608 Sir Cahir O'Doherty, a Gaelic chieftain in Inishowen, Co. Donegal, rebelled. After his defeat and execution, his lands were added to the plantation area.

PREPARATIONS ARE MADE

In 1609 English officials and soldiers travelled throughout the six counties which were to be planted. They made a detailed examination of the area and drew up maps. The maps only contained two colours. Land belonging to the Protestant Church of Ireland could not be taken over, so it was shaded in, in one colour. All other land was declared to belong to the king and was given another colour.

When the study of Ulster was completed, nearly four million acres were ready for plantation. King James himself was interested in plantations, especially the English one in the American colony of Virginia. He therefore gave his full approval to the new Ulster plantation which he hoped would place loyal Protestants in control of the area.

TEST YOUR KNOWLEDGE

1 *What counties in Ulster were taken over by James I after the Flight of the Earls?*
2 *What did James I plan to do with these counties?*
3 *What three counties were not to be included in the plantation of Ulster? Why?*
4 *How much land was to be included in the plantation?*

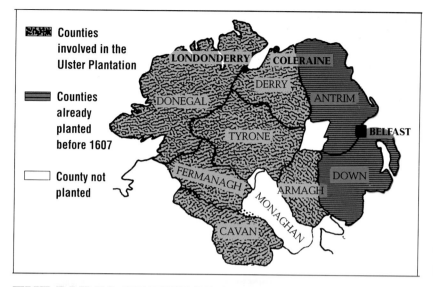

The plantation of Ulster.

Legend:
- Counties involved in the Ulster Plantation
- Counties already planted before 1607
- County not planted

Map labels: LONDONDERRY, COLERAINE, DERRY, DONEGAL, ANTRIM, TYRONE, BELFAST, FERMANAGH, ARMAGH, DOWN, MONAGHAN, CAVAN

THE RULES OF THE PLANTATION

James I and his advisers were determined to avoid the mistakes made during the earlier plantations in Laois-Offaly under Queen Mary and in Munster under Queen Elizabeth I. In both of these earlier plantations, the new English planters had brought few farmers and workers over with them. Instead, they let out farms to Irish tenants and employed Irish workers. The Ulster plantation was to be different: planters were ordered to bring over English and Scottish tenants and craftsmen to build up the new plantation.

Under the plantation rules there were three type of planter: *undertakers*, *servitors* and *Irish landowners*.

UNDERTAKERS

These were English or Scottish gentlemen who were to receive estates of 2,000 acres, 1,500 acres or 1,000 acres at a rent of £5.33 per 1,000 acres. The rent was low because of the expenses they ran up in bringing Scottish and English tenants to Ulster. They were not allowed to rent land to Irish tenants.

SERVITORS

These were men who had served the king either as soldiers or as officials. They usually got estates of 1,000 acres at a rent of £8. They were allowed to take Irish tenants.

IRISH LANDOWNERS

A small part of the land was given to Irish gentlemen who were loyal to the king. These people were removed from their old homes, however, and placed near English servitors who were to watch over them. Irish landowners were allowed to take Irish tenants and had to pay a rent of £10.66 for 1,000 acres.

The undertakers and servitors were expected to build a defensive enclosure or *bawn* to defend their settlements from attack by the Irish whose land they had taken over. Planters with 1,500 acres had to build a stone house inside the bawn. Those with 2,000 acres had to build a castle. In case of attack, the planter and his family, his tenants and their animals could shelter inside the bawn.

The Ulster plantation was started in 1609. It developed steadily and by 1618 there were about 40,000 English and Scottish settlers in Ulster. However, the plantation did not work out quite as well as the English government had hoped.

TEST YOUR KNOWLEDGE
1 *In what ways was the Ulster plantation going to be different from earlier plantations in Laois-Offaly and Munster?*
2 *Name the three types of planter to be given land.*
3 *Who were: (a) the undertakers; (b) the servitors?*
4 *How were the settlers to defend themselves against attack?*
5 *When did the Ulster plantation begin? How many settlers had arrived by 1618?*

THE PLANTATION IN ACTION

From the start the government could not persuade enough undertakers to go to Ulster. As a result, James I forced the London trade guilds to take part. These were rich groups of businessmen such as goldsmiths or cloth merchants. They were given Co. Derry at the same rent as the undertakers. These businessmen formed *The Irish Society* and let out the land to tenants. They built two towns, Coleraine and Derry (which they later named Londonderry).

The government had another problem to face as well as the shortage of undertakers. Existing undertakers were breaking the rules by renting land to Irish tenants and employing Irish workers. Irish tenants were willing to pay higher rents than English or Scots farmers. They were needed to build up the colony as there was a shortage of workers. Despite repeated warnings from the government, undertakers continued to take on Irish tenants and workers.

Conditions were harsh and dangerous for the new settlers. The Irish who had lost their lands often attacked the settlers and drove away their cattle. Travel was especially dangerous for the planters as they were liable to attack, robbery and even death when passing through wild parts of the countryside.

Most settlers lived in isolated little villages centred on the house of the planter with its protective bawn. A few workers, a teacher and a clergyman with his small church usually completed the settlement.

Some of the settlers brought a new style of living to Ulster: the life of the town.

TEST YOUR KNOWLEDGE

1. *What were the London trade guilds? What part did they play in the plantation of Ulster?*
2. *Why did the undertakers rent land to Irish tenants and employ Irish workers?*
3. *Why were conditions dangerous for the new settlers?*
4. *Where did most of the settlers live?*

THE PLANTATION TOWNS

Before the defeat of the Gaelic chieftains and the plantation of Ulster, towns were practically unknown in the province. Only Carrickfergus and Newry existed as towns in 1600. Whereas Gaelic chieftains did not build towns, the English believed that towns were centres of order and civilisation. New towns were part of the plans drawn up for the plantation of Ulster.

The plan of the plantation towns was very simple. There was a square or diamond-shaped market place in the centre where important buildings such as the church and town hall were situated. Four streets led away from the market place at right angles. As a means of defence, towns were usually surrounded by high walls or earthen banks. The new towns soon became important, as local markets, fairs and court cases were held there. The sites for the towns were carefully chosen and some of them developed into important centres of population such as Belfast, Enniskillen and Omagh.

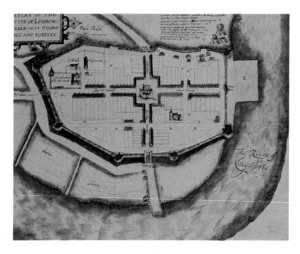

Plan of the plantation town of Londonderry.

The new Ulster towns were usually given a charter by the king which allowed them to be ruled by a council or corporation. These corporations usually contained twelve members known as *burgesses*. Burgesses had to be members of the Protestant Church of Ireland. Each year they elected one of their members to be head of the town. This man was known as the *provost* or the *sovereign*. If a burgess died, the others could elect someone to take his place. Another important privilege held by the burgesses was the right to elect members of parliament to represent the town.

TEST YOUR KNOWLEDGE
1 *What two towns existed in Ulster before the plantation?*
2 *Describe the new plantation towns.*
3 *Name three towns set up as a result of the Ulster plantation.*
4 *Who were the burgesses?*

94

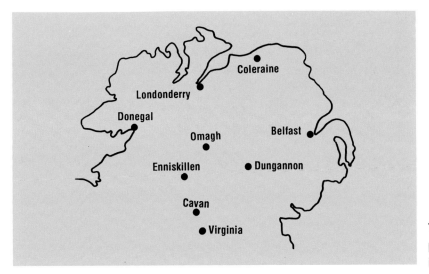

The principal plantation towns in Ulster.

THE RESULTS OF THE ULSTER PLANTATION

The Ulster plantation was the first English plantation in Ireland which was largely successful. Although many Irish people remained as tenants in the planted areas, most of the best land in the area was now in the hands of English and Scottish planters. These had succeeded in introducing the English language and English customs in Ulster. The Scottish settlers especially brought in a new way of life, completely dependent on hard work and a determination to get on in life.

The most lasting result of the Ulster plantation concerned religion. The Protestant settlers soon came to outnumber the Catholic Irish in Ulster. Most English settlers belonged to the Church of Ireland which was ruled by King James. The Scottish settlers, however, were mainly Presbyterians or followers of John Calvin. This stern religion was responsible for their hardworking lives. It was also the cause of their bitter hatred of the Catholic religion. From the time of the plantation onwards, Ulster has been divided, with the Catholic Irish on the one side and the Protestant descendants of the plantation settlers on the other.

THE PLANTATION OF ULSTER

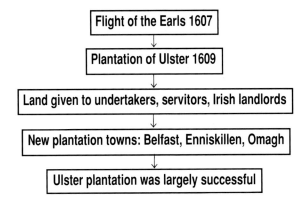

Flight of the Earls 1607
↓
Plantation of Ulster 1609
↓
Land given to undertakers, servitors, Irish landlords
↓
New plantation towns: Belfast, Enniskillen, Omagh
↓
Ulster plantation was largely successful

TEST YOUR KNOWLEDGE
1 Was the Ulster plantation a success? Explain why.
2 What customs did the settlers bring to Ulster?
3 What religious beliefs were held by the new Scottish settlers?
4 What religious divisions were created in Ulster as a result of the plantation?

Chapter 10: Review

- In 1607 the Gaelic chieftains of Ulster left Ireland for ever. This event became known as the Flight of the Earls and it prepared the way for the plantation of Ulster.

- Six of the nine counties of Ulster were taken over by the English government and a detailed survey took place in preparation for a plantation by English and Scottish settlers.

- Three types of planters arrived in Ulster: undertakers (English or Scottish gentlemen receiving estates of 2,000, 1,500 or 1,000 acres); servitors (men who had served the king as soldiers or officials); and Irish landowners who were loyal to the king.

- By 1618 there were about 40,000 English and Scottish settlers in Ulster.

However, not enough undertakers arrived. In addition, land was rented out to Irish tenants, and Irish laboure were employed. The settlers were also constantly attacked by those Gaelic Irish who had lost their land.

- Many new plantation towns were set u These included Belfast, Enniskillen a Omagh. Each town usually had a mark square in the centre. It had its own charter and was ruled by a council or corporation.

- Overall, the Ulster plantation was a success. English and Scottish customs were introduced into the area and the best land was in the hands of the settlers. As a result of the plantation, Ulster was to have deep religious divisions involving Protestants and Catholics.

ACTIVITIES

Multiple choice

(a) One of the most powerful Gaelic chieftains in Ulster was: (i) the earl of Kildare; (ii) the earl of Desmond; (iii) Hugh O'Neill; (iv) the earl of Ormond.

(b) The plantation of Ulster began after: (i) the Battle of the Yellow Ford; (ii) the Flight of the Earls; (iii) the Battle of Kinsale; (iv) the Treaty of Mellifont.

(c) The plantation of Ulster was carried out during the reign of: (i) Queen Elizabeth I; (ii) King Henry VIII; (iii) Queen Mary; (iv) King James I.

(d) Servitors were: (i) English or Scottish gentlemen; (ii) Irish landowners; (iii) men who had worked for the king either as soldiers or officials; (iv) Irish tenants who were loyal to the king.

Complete the following sentences:

(a) After the Flight of the Earls, the province of Ulster was _____.

(b) The counties settled under the plantation of Ulster were _____.

(c) King James I hoped that the Ulster plantation would place _____.

(d) Undertakers were _____.

(e) As a result of the Ulster plantation, the Protestant settlers in the province soon came to outnumber _____.

3 Write a paragraph on the Flight of the Earls.

4 Draw a map of Ulster and shade in the following:

(a) The counties involved in the plantation of Ulster (1609).

(b) Other counties which were planted.

(c) The county which was not planted.

5 List three important results of the plantation of Ulster.

IRELAND UNDER CHARLES I: A TIME OF REBELLION AND CIVIL WAR

CHARLES I AND THE GRACES

When Charles I became king on the death of his father James I in 1625, England was at war with Spain and the government was badly in need of money. Charles looked to Ireland for help and decided to approach the Catholic Old English lords and merchants. He promised that if they paid him £120,000 he would relax some of the laws against Catholics. This proposal was known as the *Graces* because the king would act 'out of his royal grace and bounty'.

There were fifty-one Graces in all. The most important ones stated that those holding government jobs need not take the oath of supremacy and that landowners who had held their estates for over sixty years would not be removed. Although the money was paid over, parliament never met to approve the Graces, and eventually Charles I cancelled them altogether after he had spent the money.

Catholics were more secure for some time after this. But the Graces episode showed the weakness of the Old English. They had been treated badly but could do very little about it. The Graces also marked a step forward on the road towards the coming together of all Catholics in Ireland, Old Irish and Old English alike.

King Charles I (1625-49).

WENTWORTH IN IRELAND

In 1633 Charles I sent one of his ablest ministers, Sir Thomas Wentworth, to Ireland as lord deputy. Wentworth was later made earl of Strafford for his services to the king while in Ireland.

On arriving in Ireland, Wentworth began at once to increase the money coming to the king through taxes and fines. The following were the main means he used:

Thomas Wentworth, earl of Strafford.

Trade was encouraged and pirates rooted out by the navy. Wentworth then increased the duties on trade and collected much higher taxes as a result.

In Ulster he stopped the export of flax and tried to make the flax growers start a linen industry at home. Although the attempt was not very successful, it was yet another effort to increase taxation by making the country richer.

Wentworth collected huge fines from large Protestant landowners who had taken over land without proper rights to it. One of these was Richard Boyle, the earl of Cork, who had to pay a huge fine and return large areas of land which he had taken illegally from the Protestant Church. The Ulster planters were another source of money. Wentworth fined undertakers who had broken the law by taking on Irish tenants. He also fined the London Irish Society which had planted Co. Londonderry. He took the county back from them and returned it to the king.

This policy of enforcing the king's rights so fully was known as *Thorough*. This was a suitable name because Wentworth was certainly 'thorough' in his efforts to raise money for Charles I in Ireland.

Wentworth's biggest plan to raise money was to start a plantation in Connaught. He claimed that all Connaught had belonged to the king for over 300 years. He then threatened Catholic landowners and forced them to hand over a quarter of their land if they wanted to hold on to the rest. This made both Old Irish and Old English landowners very worried that even more land might be taken from them in future. They therefore turned against Wentworth and longed for the day when he would leave Ireland.

The official State Church, the Protestant Church of Ireland, was in a bad state at this time. It had small congregations, many uneducated ministers and its churches were in a ruinous state. Wentworth brought about improvements in the Church because he believed that all Irish people should follow the king's religion. He did not persecute Catholics, however, because he needed their support for King Charles. He did try to impose his views on the Ulster Presbyterians by getting rid of Puritan ministers and supporting the Church of Ireland in Ulster.

In July 1639 Charles I called Wentworth back to England to help him in his struggle with the English parliament. Few people in Ireland regretted his departure. In fact he had turned three very important groups against him:

- The Protestant New English settlers, because of his strict government and the heavy fines he ha[d] imposed on some of them.
- The Ulster Presbyterians, because of his opposition to their religion.
- The Catholic Old English and Old Irish landowners, because he was a threat to their ownership of land.

Before leaving Ireland, Wentworth had raised an army of Catholics to help Charles I crush the rebellion of the English parliament. This was one of the many charges which led to his trial and execution by the English parliament in May 1641.

The execution of Wentworth in London, May 1641.

TEST YOUR KNOWLEDGE

1 Who became king of England in 1625? Why was he short of money?
2 Explain the meaning of the Graces.
3 Did the Graces succeed?
4 What was Wentworth's main concern on his arrival in Ireland as lord deputy in 1633?
5 Explain Wentworth's policy of Thorough.
6 What plans had he for Connaught?
7 How did Wentworth improve the Protestant Church of Ireland?
8 Why did Charles I recall Wentworth to England in 1639?
9 What happened to him on his return to England?

REBELLION BREAKS OUT IN ULSTER

The death of Wentworth, the king's strongest ruler in Ireland, was seen by the Irish in Ulster as a chance to rise up in arms and expel the English and Scots planters from the province. Ever since the plantation of Ulster in 1609, they had been waiting for a chance to win back the lands they had lost. The rebellion was arranged to take place in Dublin and Ulster. Led by Sir Phelim O'Neill, Rory O'More and Lord Connor Maguire, the rebels planned to capture Dublin Castle. This plot was revealed to the government by spies and the rebels failed to capture Dublin. The rising went ahead as planned in Ulster, however.

23 October 1641 was chosen as the date for the rebellion. On that day beacon fires were lit all over the province as a sign that the rising was to begin. Throughout the planted lands, English and Scots planters and their families were attacked by the native Irish rebels. Over 10,000 settlers were killed and many more fled for safety to the walled towns of Ulster. Richer settlers were able to flee to Scotland and England, where they told stories of attacks and massacres carried out by the Irish rebels.

In England and Scotland there was widespread outrage at the sufferings of Protestants in Ulster. Exaggerated stories were passed around. Some writers claimed that 300,000 Protestants had been slaughtered, about thirty times the true figure. A pamphlet called *The Irish Rebellion* by Sir William Temple contained these exaggerations and it was believed by English readers for many years to come.

Phelim O'Neill, er of the llion in Ulster 641.

Sr Phillom O Neale heife Traytor of all Ireland.

A Protestant artist's view of the sufferings of fellow Protestants in Ulster during the rebellion of 1641.

In England and Scotland two attempts were made to put down the rebellion in Ulster.

- The Scottish parliament sent 10,000 soldiers under General Monro to defend the Protestant settlers in Ulster.
- The English parliament tried to raise money to send an army to Ireland by passing the Adventurers' Act. This promised Irish land to anyone who contributed money towards an army to put down rebellion in Ireland. The men who paid out money in this way were known as English adventurers.

Because King Charles I and the English parliament were close to going to war against each other, they could not do much to change the situation in Ireland. By the end of 1641 all of Ulster except the walled towns and much of Leinster were in the hands of the rebels – and the government of Charles I in Dublin was rapidly losing control of the country.

OLD IRISH AND OLD ENGLISH UNITE

At this time the Catholic Old English lords and merchants were faced with a very difficult choice. Should they support the Protestant king and parliament in England, or should they unite instead with their fellow Catholics, the Old Irish? The Old English leaders knew that if the English parliament defeated Charles I, they would be harshly treated because they were Catholics. Therefore in November 1641 at Drogheda the Old English of the Pale made an alliance with the rebel Old Irish in defence of the Catholic faith. They insisted, however, that the Old Irish should agree with them to remain loyal to King Charles I. Despite the disappointment over the Graces they were still loyal to the king; at least he would be kinder to them than the Puritans who controlled the English parliament! They also knew that their own lands were promised to English adventurers. By February 1642 nearly all of Ireland outside Dublin and the Ulster towns was in the hands of the Old Irish and Old English rebels. To rule this area they set up their own special type of government in the ancient city of Kilkenny.

TEST YOUR KNOWLEDGE
1 *Why did rebellion break out in Ulster in October 1641?*
2 *Name two leaders of the rebellion.*
3 *Where did the Ulster planters flee for safety when attacked?*
4 *What legends about the Ulster massacres spread to England?*
5 *Name the general sent from Scotland to protect the settlers in Ulster.*
6 *What was the Adventurers' Act (1642)?*
7 *Why did the Old Irish and Old English forces unite in November 1641?*
8 *Why were the Old English loyal to the king of England?*

THE CONFEDERATION OF KILKENNY

The rebels called themselves the Confederate Catholics of Ireland and chose Kilkenny as their headquarters because Dublin remained in government control. The Old English chose the word 'confederation' or alliance, in case 'parliament' would offend King Charles I.

The motto of the Confederation of Kilkenny was *Pro Deo, pro rege, pro patria Hibernia unanimis*, a Latin expression meaning 'we are united for God, for the king and for Ireland our fatherland'. The Confederation was certainly not united, however. Soon the two main groups began to quarrel.

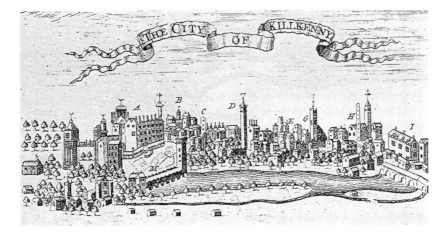

The city of Kilkenny, capital of the alliance of Old English and Gaelic Irish Catholics known as the Confederation of Kilkenny.

THE OLD IRISH

They were not really loyal to Charles I. They wanted to recover all the land lost in plantations and they expected to see the Catholic religion recognised as the official or State religion in Ireland.

THE OLD ENGLISH

They were loyal to Charles I and would have liked an alliance with him against the English parliament. They did not want all plantation lands returned – merely that no new plantation should take place. They were happy to accept freedom to practise the Catholic religion and allow Protestants the freedom to practise their own religion as well.

St Canice's Cathedral, Kilkenny, where members of the Confederation frequently met.

In 1642 nearly all Ireland, except for the shaded areas and some towns, was under Confederate control.

The political divisions within the Confederation also led to a division in the army:

- The Old Irish army in Ulster was led by Owen Roe O'Neill, a nephew of the great Hugh O'Neill. Owen Roe returned from the Spanish army to fight for the Confederation.
- The Old English army in Leinster was under the command of Colonel Thomas Preston, a brother of Lord Gormanston and one of the leading Old English lords of the Pale.

The Confederation of Kilkenny hoped to gain help from the Catholic countries in Europe. However, the only assistance came from the pope, who sent his own representative in 1645.

RINUCCINI IN IRELAND

In October 1645 Archbishop John Baptist Rinuccini arrived in Ireland. He was the *papal nuncio* or the pope's representative. He landed in Kenmare, Co. Kerry, with supplies and money for the Confederate forces. Rinuccini had been instructed by the pope to encourage the Catholics of the Confederation of Kilkenny to continue their rebellion against the Protestant English king and parliament. He was not, however, to involve himself in political matters.

Rinuccini forgot this piece of advice and soon began to support the Old Irish against the Old English in the Confederation of Kilkenny. Instead of healing divisions, he made them worse. By the time he left Ireland in February 1649, the Confederation of Kilkenny was close to breaking up completely.

Owen Roe O'Ne[ill] commander of t[he] Gaelic Irish armies.

Archbishop John Baptist Rinuccini who was sent by the pope as papal nuncio to Ireland in 1645.

THE PROGRESS OF THE WAR

In June 1646 Owen Roe O'Neill had won a massive victory over General Monro at the Battle of Benburb in Ulster. The Confederate forces failed to follow up this success, and in August 1647 Colonel Preston was defeated by a parliamentary army at the Battle of Dungan's Hill in Meath. In the following November the Confederation suffered a huge defeat in Munster when the parliamentary leader, Lord Inchiquin, won the Battle of Knockanoss in Co. Cork. To add to the misfortunes of the Confederation, the earl of Ormond, who had held Dublin for Charles I, fled abroad, but handed the city over to the control of the English parliament.

The earl of Ormond, Charles I's last lord deputy in Ireland.

THE VICTORY OF THE ENGLISH PARLIAMENT

In January 1649 King Charles I was beheaded by the English parliament. Having won the Civil War in England, the parliamentary leaders now looked to Ireland and planned to gain complete control there.

The execution of Charles I gained his followers widespread sympathy in Ireland. The earl of Ormond returned, Lord Inchiquin changed sides, and together they led an army against the parliamentary forces. On 2 August 1649 they were defeated by a parliamentary army under Michael Jones at the Battle of Rathmines in Co. Dublin. This cleared the way for the arrival in Dublin thirteen days later of the leader of the English parliament: *Oliver Cromwell.*

1 How did the Confederation of Kilkenny come into being?
2 What was its motto?
3 List the main aims of the Old Irish.
4 What were the main aims of the Old English?
5 Name the general who led the Old Irish army.
6 Name the general who led the Old English army of the Pale.
7 Who was the papal nuncio sent by the pope to the Confederation of Kilkenny in 1645?
8 Why did his mission fail?
9 Who led the victorious Irish army at the Battle of Benburb (1646)?
10 Who handed the city of Dublin over to the control of the English parliament?
11 What happened at the Battle of Rathmines (1649)?

Chapter 11: Review

- When Charles I became king in 1625 he was short of money and hoped to raise large sums from the Old English lords and merchants in Ireland by offering them relief from the penal laws against Catholics. This offer was known as the Graces.

- In 1633 Charles I sent Sir Thomas Wentworth to Ireland as lord deputy with the main aim of raising higher taxes for the king's exchequer. Wentworth raised customs duties and imposed heavy fines on rich landowners.

- Wentworth's biggest plan was a proposed plantation in Connaught. This made the Old English very uneasy because they feared they would lose their land.

- Before leaving Ireland Wentworth raised an army of Irish Catholics to help Charles I against the English parliament. This was one of the main charges which led to his trial and execution by the parliament in 1641.

- The Old Irish under Sir Phelim O'Neill broke out in rebellion in Ulster in October 1641. Scots and English settlers were attacked and had to flee t the walled towns for safety.

- General Monro arrived from Scotland with 10,000 men to protect the settler: in Ulster. The English parliament passed the Adventurers' Act (1642) to raise money for the war in Ireland.

- In November 1641 the Old English an Old Irish joined forces at Drogheda. By the spring of 1642 they controlled mos of Ireland except Dublin and the walle towns in Ulster. They set up their headquarters at Kilkenny and formed a alliance known as the Confederation of Kilkenny. However, the Confederation was far from united.

- While the Old Irish were not really loyal to Charles I and wanted all plantations overturned, the Old English were loyal to the king and would be satisfied if no new plantation took place.

- The Old Irish army in Ulster was unde the command of Owen Roe O'Neill, while the Old English army in Leinster was led by Colonel Thomas Preston.

In 1645 the pope sent Archbishop Rinuccini as papal nuncio to Ireland. Rinuccini involved himself in political quarrels and made divisions within the Confederation worse by siding with the Old Irish against the Old English. He left Ireland in 1649 after failing in his mission.

In June 1646 Owen Roe O'Neill won a massive victory over General Monro at the Battle of Benburb. However, the victory was not followed up, and in 1647 the Confederate forces suffered a number of defeats.

- In January 1649 Charles I was executed in London. In August a parliamentary army under Michael Jones defeated the Royalist forces at Rathmines outside Dublin. This cleared the way for the arrival of Oliver Cromwell, the English parliamentary leader. He arrived in Dublin thirteen days later.

ACTIVITIES

True or false?
(a) The Graces were gifts of money given to King Charles I by Catholics in Ireland.
(b) In 1633 Charles I sent Thomas Wentworth as lord deputy to Ireland.
(c) The Irish forces suffered a heavy defeat at the Battle of Benburb in 1646.
(d) In October 1641 a rebellion broke out in Connaught.
(e) In 1642 the various Catholic groups in Ireland formed the Confederation of Kilkenny.

Complete the following sentences:
(a) In 1645 the pope sent a representative to Ireland. His name was _____.
(b) During the rebellion in Ulster in 1641 there were massacres of _____.
(c) There were divisions at the Confederation of Kilkenny between the Old English and _____.
(d) The Irish leader at the Battle of Benburb was _____.
(e) In August 1649 the leader of the English parliament landed in Dublin. His name was _____.

Describe the career of Thomas Wentworth in Ireland.

Imagine that you were a settler fleeing to save your life in Ulster in 1641. Describe the events which you witnessed.

Write a paragraph on the Confederation of Kilkenny.

CHAPTER 12

THE CROMWELLIAN PLANTATION

CROMWELL ARRIVES IN IRELAND

On 13 August 1649 Oliver Cromwell and his army of 12,000 experienced soldiers landed at Ringsend near Dublin. He did not remain in Dublin, but set out with his army for Drogheda. This important town blocked the way to Ulster.

Cromwell's capture of Drogheda and the massacre which followed blackened his name in Ireland for ever. Read the following account of Cromwell's capture of Drogheda. It was written by an English army officer.

WORKING WITH EVIDENCE

After landing at Ringsend, Cromwell marched into Dublin and gathered his army together at Oxmantown Green, just north of the river Liffey. He then marched to Drogheda in order to capture it for the English Commonwealth.

As soon as Cromwell came before the walls of Drogheda, he sent his trumpet player to sound an alarm and call on those inside to surrender up the town. But they answered no, that until they lost their lives they would not hand over the king's soldiers to such a notorious enemy of His Majesty.

After this Cromwell ordered his troops to bombard the walls of the town with cannon fire. After a few days they made a breach in the wall at the south side of the town. Twice Cromwell's men tried to enter through this breach but were beaten back with great loss. At a third attempt, Cromwell himself led them and they succeeded in entering this time but had to fight hard in the streets.

Once the Irish were defeated they were all cut down and killed and no mercy was shown to man, woman or child for twenty-four hours. Not a dozen people escaped out of Drogheda, townspeople or soldiers.

After he captured Drogheda, Cromwell marched south to capture the rest of the country.

1 *What did Cromwell do after landing at Ringsend?*
2 *Describe Cromwell's actions on reaching the walls of Drogheda.*
3 *Why did the defenders of Drogheda refuse to surrender?*
4 *How did Cromwell's army eventually capture the town?*
5 *Describe the massacre which followed.*
6 *What did Cromwell and his army do after capturing Drogheda?*

ver
omwell, the
rd Protector
England,
ded at
ngsend near
blin in
gust 1649
h an army of
,000
perienced
diers.

CROMWELL CAPTURES THE REST OF IRELAND

When news reached other towns of Cromwell's actions in Drogheda, their people surrendered to avoid massacre. Take a close look at the map to see how the rest of Ireland was brought under Cromwell's control.

With Ireland conquered, it now remained for Cromwell and the English parliament to decide what to do with the country.

Cromwell attacking the town of Drogheda.

Cromwell's campaign in Ireland.

THE CROMWELLIAN PLANTATION

By 1652 Ireland was a country worn out by ten years of warfare. Famine and plague were widespread. Wolves roamed the countryside and even came into the neighbourhood of the towns in search of food.

Because so many men had died in the war, and with many Irish soldiers going overseas, large numbers of women and children were unprovided for. The English government had these rounded up and sold as slaves to work in the sugar plantations in the West Indies.

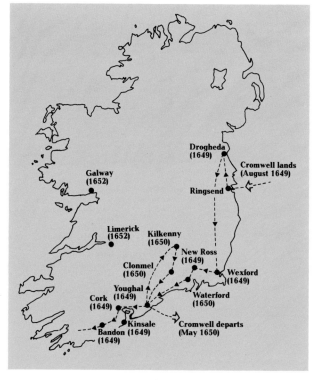

109

Some Catholic priests were also transported to the West Indies. Many more were executed. Anyone who handed over a priest to the authorities was paid a reward of £5. Cromwell and the government hoped that the Catholic religion would die out in Ireland from lack of priests. However, many priests remained in Ireland, where they disguised themselves as lay people. They said mass in the houses of the rich Catholics or in desolate places hidden away in the countryside.

Catholics prayed in the open air when they were not allowed the freedom to practise their religion during Cromwell's rule.

Cromwell's principal method of gaining control of Ireland, however, was to be a new plantation. He believed in clearing most of the country of Catholic landowners and of Protestant landowners who remained loyal to the king. He decided to give the land to Englishmen who supported the parliament and to soldiers who had fought for him in the Civil War. Cromwell also needed the land to pay the adventurers who had given money to the English parliament in exchange for promises of land in Ireland.

Before a new plantation could take place, however, the land had first to be surveyed and mapped.

SIR WILLIAM PETTY AND THE DOWN SURVEY

In 1653 mapmakers accompanied by soldiers travelled throughout the country, questioning local people, measuring the land and drawing up maps. Progress was very slow, however, and those expecting grants of land in the plantation began to complain.

In 1654 Sir William Petty, a thirty-one-year-old army doctor, offered to complete the survey in thirteen months at a lower cost. His offer was accepted by the government and the result was the *Down Survey*, so named simply because the results were written down! Petty's surveyors were guarded by armed soldiers to protect them from the *tories* or Irish outlaws. Despite all obstacles, the Down Survey was completed on time and Petty was richly rewarded for his work. As well as his fee of over £18,000 he also gained a vast estate near Kenmare in Co. Kerry.

The Down Survey maps were the most accurate to be produced in Ireland up until that time. They were the best maps available until Ordnance Survey maps appeared in the 1840s.

Now that the country was surveyed and mapped, Cromwell's government was ready to go ahead with the plantation.

TEST YOUR KNOWLEDGE
1   *Why were large numbers of women and children left unprovided for in Ireland in 1652?*
2   *How did the government deal with these people?*
3   *What reward was paid to those who handed over Catholic priests to the authorities?*
4   *Did Cromwell's government succeed in getting rid of all Catholic priests from Ireland?*
5   *What landowners did Cromwell wish to clear from their lands?*
6   *Why did he need land in Ireland?*
7   *Who was Sir William Petty? With what is his name associated?*
8   *Why was the Down Survey given its name?*
9   *Who were the tories in the 1650s?*

'TO HELL OR TO CONNAUGHT'

Most of Munster, Leinster and Connaught were taken over by Cromwell's government because the landowners in these provinces had fought against the English parliament. Under the Act of Settlement (1652) leaders of the rebellion were to lose their lands, along with their lives. Those who could not prove that they had been loyal to the parliament were to lose part of their lands. They were also to be transplanted to Connaught where they could exchange their old estates for poorer new lands.

All transplanted landowners were ordered to be west of the river Shannon by May 1654. This gave rise to the saying 'to hell or to Connaught'. They were to be kept in Connaught behind the barrier of the Shannon. There was to be a mile-wide stretch along the Shannon and the west coast reserved for soldiers. This was designed as a means of providing security against the Irish landowners.

Only the landowners were ordered to Connaught. Ordinary farmers and labourers remained behind to work for their new English landlords.

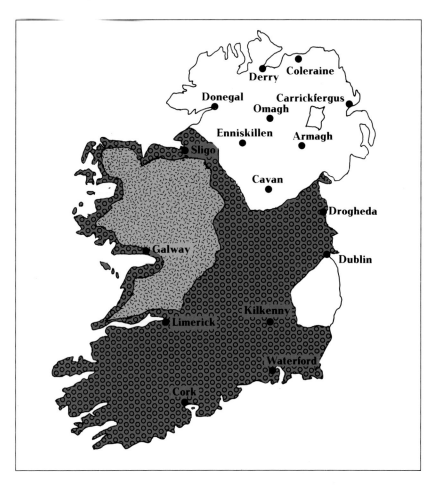

Areas given by Cromwell to new landowners

Area reserved for transplanted Irish landowners

The Cromwellian plantation of Ireland.

THE RESULTS OF THE CROMWELLIAN PLANTATION

The Cromwellian plantation did not work out as well as Cromwell and the English government had hoped:

- Many English adventurers never came to live on their estates but sold them to rich landlords.
- Many soldier-settlers married Catholic women and their children were brought up as Catholics.
- Tories and other Irish outlaws frequently attacked the new planters.

Despite these setbacks, the Cromwellian plantation had important long-term effects on land ownership:

- Before 1641 Catholic landowners owned large parts of Munster, Connaught and Leinster. After the plantation, Catholics were confined to the poorer land west of the Shannon.
- Many of the new landowners and their descendants were absentees. They lived in England where they spent the rent collected from their estates.
- All land and property in the towns was taken from Catholics and transferred to Protestants.
- Catholics lost all positions on town councils. This situation was to last for nearly 200 years.

Although not the largest of the plantations, the Cromwellian plantation had the greatest long-term effect on land ownership. As a result of the changes which it brought about, Ireland became a land deeply divided between Protestant landlords and Catholic tenants for the next two centuries.

TEST YOUR KNOWLEDGE
1 Explain the Act of Settlement (1652).
2 What is meant by the saying 'to hell or to Connaught'?
3 List two threats to the success of the plantation.
4 What effect had the plantation on Catholic landowners?
5 What is meant by absentees?
6 Explain how Cromwell's government changed the conditions of Catholics in towns.

Chapter 12: Review

For thirty years after the Ulster plantation, there were peaceful conditions throughout Ireland. In 1641, however, a rebellion broke out in Ulster and throughout Ireland.

Because many Protestant settlers were massacred in Ulster during the rebellion of 1641, English Protestant leaders planned to gain revenge. Their opportunity arrived when the new ruler of England, Oliver Cromwell, arrived in Ireland with a large army in 1649.

After his arrival in Dublin, Cromwell marched to the town of Drogheda, where he carried out a massacre of the townspeople.

Frightened by the news from Drogheda, people in the rest of Ireland soon surrendered to Cromwell's armies.

By 1652 Ireland was a country worn out by ten years of warfare and on the brink of starvation. Cromwell now tried to wipe out the Catholic religion in Ireland by executing or transporting many Catholic priests.

- Plantation was the main method used by Cromwell to control Ireland. He decided to give Irish lands to Englishmen who supported the parliament and to soldiers who had fought for him in the Civil War.

- In 1654 Sir William Petty surveyed and mapped the area to be 'planted'. His work was called the Down Survey. His maps were the most accurate yet produced in Ireland.

- Most of Munster, Leinster and Connaught were to be taken over by Cromwell's government for the plantation. All those evicted from their land were ordered to be west of the Shannon by May 1654. Those who lost their land included Old English as well as Gaelic Irish.

- The Cromwellian plantation did not work out as well as expected. Many English adventurers never came to live on their estates; many soldier-settlers married Catholic women. At the same time, however, the plantation brought about major changes in land ownership.

ACTIVITIES

1 *Fill in the blanks with the words from the box.*

Petty	**Drogheda**	**Connaught**	**Catholic**	**Ringsend**	**Protestant**

In August 1649 Oliver Cromwell landed with a huge army at _____. He then set out for _____, where his army massacred the people of the town. When news of this reached people in other towns, they opened the gates to Cromwell's soldiers. Cromwell hoped that the _____ religion would die out in Ireland. He planned to give land in Ireland to his loyal _____ followers. In 1654 a young doctor named _____ agreed to complete a survey of Ireland for Cromwell's government. When the plantation took place, most Irish landowners were transported to the province of _____.

2 *Study the maps of Ireland carefully and then answer the questions which follow.*
(a) Which plantation took place at A?
(b) Name the Gaelic clans who lost their lands in this plantation.
(c) Who ruled England when this plantation took place?
(d) Name the plantation which took place at B.
(e) Who was the ruler of England at the time?
(f) Name two Englishmen who were given large estates there.
(g) Name the plantation at C. State who ruled England when it took place.
(h) What was the plantation shown at D?

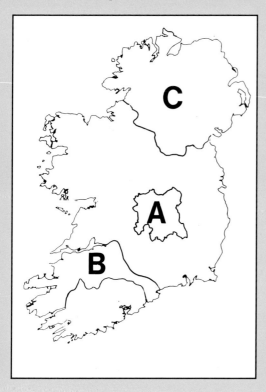
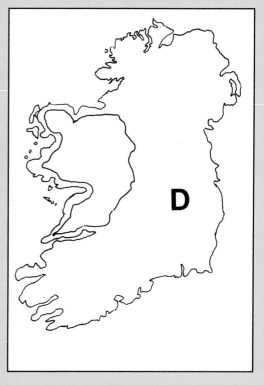

3 Study this chart on the changes in land ownership in Ireland between 1603 and 1700. Then answer the questions which follow.
(a) In 1603 what percentage of land was owned by: (i) Catholics; (ii) Protestants?
(b) In 1700 what percentage of land was owned by; (i) Catholics; (ii) Protestants?
(c) Explain the reason for the changes noted in (a) and (b) above.

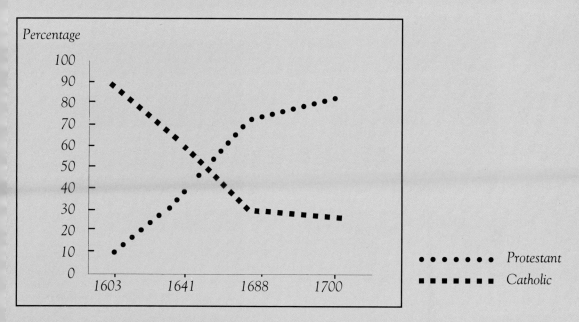

4 Choose: (a) a successful plantation; (b) an unsuccessful plantation. In the case of (a), state why the plantation succeeded. In the case of (b), explain why the plantation failed.

CHAPTER 13

THE WAR OF THE THREE KINGS

THE RESTORATION OF KING CHARLES II

In May 1660 King Charles II, the son of the executed Charles I, returned from exile in Europe to become ruler of England, Scotland, Wales and Ireland. Most people regarded the return of the king as a welcome change from the harsh government of Cromwell and his Puritan followers.

The new king had a very different personality from that of his father, Charles I. Whereas his father had been stubborn and uncompromising, Charles II was willing to follow the advice of others in order to remain on the throne. He had far less power than previous kings of England. As a result of the Civil War the parliament was much stronger, and Charles II had to accept whatever laws were passed there.

Charles II
(1660-85).

In Ireland the restoration of Charles II was welcomed by many lords, both Catholic and Protestant, who had supported his father in the Civil War. They had then lost their land during the Cromwellian plantation and now hoped that the new king would restore them. However, some of the most powerful men who arranged for the return of Charles II were former Cromwellian supporters. The king was too weak to oppose these, and as a result there was little change in land ownership in Ireland during the reign of Charles II.

Catholics in particular felt angry at the government of Charles II. Many Catholic lords had supported Charles I and Charles II against Cromwell and they got little reward for their loyalty. Although penal laws against them were eased somewhat there were occasional outbreaks of persecution. The worst of these was the so-called *Popish Plot*, a fictitious story invented by Titus Oates, who claimed that Catholics in England and Ireland were planning to murder Charles II. As a result of the hysteria whipped up between 1678 and 1681 a number of Catholic priests were executed. The most famous victim of

116

the Popish Plot was Oliver Plunkett, the Catholic Archbishop of Armagh, who was executed in London in July 1681. It was believed that Charles II opposed the execution but he was too weak to prevent it.

However, Catholics in Ireland and England had high hopes of a better future. The heir of Charles II was his younger brother, James Duke of York, who had become a Catholic and had married an Italian Catholic princess, Mary of Modena.

As Charles II grew older Catholics became more hopeful, while Protestants in England and Ireland grew fearful of the consequences of having a Catholic sovereign for the first time since Queen Mary Tudor (1553-58). To understand Protestant fears we must take a brief look at the most powerful Catholic ruler in Europe at the time, King Louis XIV of France.

Oliver Plunkett, the Catholic Archbishop of Armagh executed in London in July 1681.

LOUIS XIV OF FRANCE: THE SUN KING

We have seen already how the events in Europe could have an important influence on developments in Ireland. During the sixteenth century, Spain, the most powerful country on the continent, intervened on more than one occasion in the wars between Queen Elizabeth I and the Gaelic chieftains.

However, after 1600 the power of Spain declined considerably. Between 1618 and 1648 the Great Powers of Europe were involved in a prolonged religious and political conflict known as the *Thirty Years War*. As England remained out of this conflict none of the European powers considered interfering in Ireland.

In the aftermath of the Thirty Years War, France replaced Spain as the most powerful country in Europe. Under its most powerful king ever, Louis XIV (1643-1715) it became a serious threat to its neighbours, Protestant and Catholic alike.

Known as the Sun King from the splendour of his court at Versailles, Louis XIV believed, like Charles I of England, in a theory called the *Divine Right of Kings*. According to this a king had absolute power and no parliament could question his decisions. However, whereas Charles I of England lost his life trying to put this into practice, Louis XIV of France was an all-powerful absolute monarch whose every word was law.

Believing that all French people should follow his own Catholic beliefs, Louis XIV began a campaign of persecution against French Protestants or Huguenots. In 1685 he revoked the Edict of Nantes (1598) which had guaranteed their rights. Thousands of them fled to refuge in Protestant-controlled lands such as England, Ireland, the

Louis XIV of France (1643-1715).

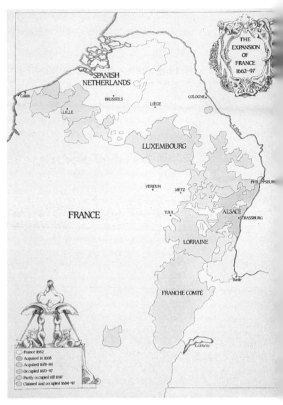

The expansion of France under Louis XIV.

Netherlands and parts of Germany. As Huguenots were excellent craftsmen and businessmen Louis XIV did serious damage to the French economy.

Among Protestants throughout Europe Louis XIV became a hated figure. Many Protestant cartoons of the period showed him dressed as the devil.

In England and Ireland Protestants awaited the death of Charles II with growing anxiety. At the back of their minds they feared that their rights and privileges would be at risk under a Catholic king.

TEST YOUR KNOWLEDGE

1 *Why did most people welcome the restoration of Charles II in 1660?*
2 *How did he differ from his father, Charles I?*
3 *Did the government of Charles II make any changes in land ownership in Ireland? Explain your answer.*
4 *Explain 'The Popish Plot'.*
5 *Who was the heir of King Charles II?*
6 *What was King Louis XIV of France known as?*
7 *Explain the theory of the Divine Right of Kings.*
8 *How did Louis XIV treat the Huguenots or French Protestants?*

JAMES II BECOMES KING

On 6 February 1685 Charles II died and was succeeded by his brother, the Catholic James II. James was to prove himself a stubborn and uncompromising ruler, much more like his father, Charles I, than his brother, Charles II. From the start of his reign James did very little to ease the fears of his Protestant subjects. He pushed forward measures to relieve the penal laws against Catholics and ignored advice to move more cautiously. He further alienated the Protestant majority in England by imprisoning seven Church of England bishops in the Tower of London for refusing to support his removal of the penal laws.

Protestants feared that James was too close to his cousin, the powerful King Louis XIV of France. However, they were prepared to wait before taking action against James because his heirs were two Protestant daughters, Mary and Anne, born during his first marriage. The elder, Mary, was the wife of Prince William of Orange, the ruler of the Netherlands. William was the greatest enemy of Louis XIV of France and a serious obstacle to his plans to expand French power.

For years William of Orange had been organising leagues of various European States to oppose Louis XIV. In May 1688 he succeeded in forming the *Grand Alliance* against the Sun King. At this stage William did not seek to remove his father-in-law from the throne of England; he merely wished to break any alliance between James II and Louis XIV. However, on 10 June 1688 an event took place which changed the course of history. James II's wife, Mary of Modena, gave birth to a son in London. The new prince replaced his sister, Mary of Orange, as heir to

es II.

Family tree of houses of Stuart and Orange.

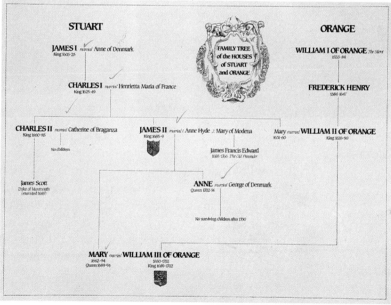

the throne. As he was baptised a Catholic Protestants now feared the prospect of a succession of Catholic kings of England.

Plans were set in motion to force James II to flee from England and to invite William and Mary of Orange to become rulers instead.

Meanwhile James II had been building up his power in the country most likely to support him: Ireland.

IRELAND UNDER JAMES II

As in England, James II lost no time in removing the penal laws against Catholics. In June 1686 he appointed the Catholic Richard Talbot, earl of Tyrconnell, to command the army in Ireland. Protestant officers and soldiers were rapidly replaced by Catholics. At the same time Catholics gained control of many Church of Ireland cathedrals and churches, and a Catholic was appointed provost or president of Trinity College, Dublin. At the same time some of the leading Protestant judges were replaced by Catholic ones.

The earl of Tyrconnell.

A Protestant vi of the birth of James II's son June 1688.

Protestants in particular mistrusted Tyrconnell, and their fears were aggravated when he was appointed viceroy of Ireland in February 1687. Richer Protestants feared that their land would be confiscated to reward James's Catholic followers. In Ulster Presbyterians were deeply suspicious of James II. While he allowed freedom of worship to Catholics he had a record of persecuting Presbyterians in Scotland. The Presbyterians in Ulster were one of the first groups in England, Scotland or Ireland to consider the replacement of James II by William and Mary of Orange.

The arrival of William of Orange in England in November 1688.

THE ARRIVAL OF WILLIAM OF ORANGE IN ENGLAND AND THE FLIGHT OF JAMES II

After the birth of his son and heir in June 1688, support for James II began to crumble. At the same time leading English politicians from both the Whig and Tory parties sent messages inviting William of Orange to invade England. As a member of the Grand Alliance William was in quite a strong position to do so. In September 1688 Louis XIV made the mistake of invading the German Rhineland. With French troops tied up in Germany the way was clear for William to invade England. He landed at Torbay in Devon on 5 November 1688 and marched towards London.

Finding himself with little support left, James II succeeded in fleeing from England on 23 December. He escaped to France to seek the assistance of his cousin and ally, Louis XIV. Together they planned an invasion of Ireland, which they saw as a stepping stone on the way to James's recovery of the throne of England.

With James removed, the parliament of England declared the throne vacant and invited William and Mary to become rulers. At the same time a *Bill of Rights* was passed, strengthening the power of parliament and reducing that of the king. These events were known as the *Glorious Revolution* and completed the process begun during the English Civil War. From then on the king had very little power, and the rich lords who controlled parliament were the real rulers of England.

The focus of the struggle turned once more to Ireland in March 1689 when James II landed with an army at Kinsale, Co. Cork, determined to reconquer his three kingdoms of England, Scotland and Ireland.

King William III (1688-1702).

Queen Mary (1688–94).

THE SIEGE OF LONDONDERRY

On the arrival of James in Ireland, most of the country was under the control of the Catholic armies led by his viceroy, the earl of Tyrconnell. However, the city of Londonderry in Ulster refused to admit an army loyal to James and its inhabitants declared themselves loyal to William of Orange. On 18 December 1688 a group of *Apprentice Boys* locked the gates against the advancing Catholic army. Despite several series of negotiations the citizens of Derry refused to admit a Jacobite army, and when James II himself appeared outside the walls on 18 April 1689 he was fired upon and some of his followers were killed.

Before 1688 the population of the town was about 2,000. During the siege about 30,000 people had crowded in there for protection. Memories were still strong concerning the rising of 1641 and many Protestants feared a repetition of the massacres which had taken place then.

A tapestry showing the Siege of Londonderry.

The besieging Jacobite forces, which numbered around 20,000 men, took up their positions on the hills surrounding the walled town. For month after month the siege continued. Conditions inside the walls became desperate as starvation, disease and the effect of mortar-bomb injuries killed thousands of people. Dogs, cats and rats were all sold as items of food during the siege. The besieging army also suffered heavy losses due to cold, lack of food and proper medical care.

Finally on 28 July 1689 the siege was broken when Williamite ships from England succeeded in breaking through the boom or obstacle on the river Foyle and bringing food to the starving inhabitants. There was a huge celebration in the city, and three days later the Jacobite forces marched away as they realised that the siege was over. It had lasted in all for 105 days.

The relief of Londonderry was a great boost to the Williamite cause. The failure to capture both Derry and Enniskillen was a serious blow to James II and his followers. As a result they abandoned most of Ulster to the Williamites. James had hoped to send forces to England and Scotland. These hopes were now dashed. At the same time as the relief of Derry the Jacobite leader in Scotland, Viscount Dundee, was killed at the Battle of Killiecrankie. The initiative now lay with William of Orange, who began to gather a vast army for an invasion of Ireland.

1 *What occurred in Londonderry on 18 December 1688?*
2 *Explain what happened to James II when he appeared outside its gates in April 1689.*
3 *What was the great fear facing the Protestants who crowded into the town?*
4 *Describe conditions inside the walls during the Siege of Derry.*
5 *How was the siege broken?*
6 *Name the other major town in Ulster which was not captured by the Jacobites.*

Chapter 13: Review

- In May 1660 King Charles II returned from exile to become ruler of Great Britain and Ireland. This event was known as the Restoration.

- Charles II had to follow the advice of parliament in ruling his kingdoms. He was supported in Ireland by some of the leading men in Cromwell's government.

- During the reign of Charles II a persecution of Catholics took place at the time of the so-called Popish Plot. One of the victims was the Archbishop of Armagh, Oliver Plunkett.

- The most powerful Catholic ruler in Europe at the time was Louis XIV of France (1643-1715), a cousin of King Charles II.

- Known as the Sun King, Louis XIV expanded French territory by fighting many wars. However, he persecuted the French Protestants or Huguenots and was hated and feared in Protestant countries like England and the Netherlands.

- In February 1685 Charles II died and was succeeded as king by his Catholic brother, the Duke of York, who became James II.

- James II began to end the penal laws against Catholics but his stubborn personality and lack of patience frightened many English Protestants.

- When a son was born to Queen Mary, the wife of James II, in June 1688 Protestants in England began to plot to invite James's Protestant daughter, Mary, and her husband, Prince William of Orange, to come to England as ruler instead of James.

- Meanwhile James II had been building up support in Ireland. He appointed a Catholic, Richard Talbot, earl of Tyrconnell, as viceroy, and Catholics were promoted as judges and army officers.

- In November 1688 William of Orange landed in England and in the following month James II fled to France. In an event known as the Glorious Revolution William and Mary replaced James and became rulers of England.

- In March 1689 James II landed at Kinsale, Co. Cork with an army of French soldiers to begin his attempt to reconquer England and Scotland.

etween December 1688 and July 1689
long siege took place at Londonderry
here Protestant inhabitants and
efugees were surrounded by the
Catholic army of James II.

- After months of severe hardship and endurance the siege was broken in July 1689. The lifting of the Siege of Londonderry was a major victory for the followers of William of Orange in Ireland.

ACTIVITIES

Multiple choice.
(a) *James II's viceroy in Ireland was the earl of: (i) Dundee; (ii) Tyrconnell; (iii) Londonderry; (iv) Drogheda.*
(b) *Huguenots were: (i) soldiers of Charles II; (ii) French soldiers in the army of James II; (iii) Protestant volunteers at the Siege of Londonderry; (iv) French Protestants expelled by Louis XIV.*
(c) *The Glorious Revolution took place when: (i) Protestants rebelled against Louis XIV; (ii) Ulster Protestants captured Carrickfergus; (iii) William and Mary became rulers of Great Britain and Ireland; (iv) Scottish Presbyterians defeated the forces of Charles II.*
(d) *The other major Ulster town along with Londonderry which the Jacobites failed to capture was: (i) Enniskillen; (ii) Omagh; (iii) Carrickfergus; (iv) Monaghan.*

Fill in the blanks with words from the box.

Jacobite   starvation   boom   Foyle   siege   Apprentice   Williamite   massacres

The _____ of Londonderry began in December 1688 when the _____ Boys locked the gate in the face of _____ soldiers. Many Protestants feared a repetition of the _____ of 1641. After months of hardship including conditions of _____ the siege was broken in July 1689 when _____ ships broke through the _____ on the river _____ and brought food to the starving inhabitants.

3 *Draw up a time chart of the main events in England and Ireland between the death of Charles II in February 1685 and the Relief of Londonderry in July 1689.*

4 *Imagine that you were present at the Siege of Londonderry either as (a) a citizen inside the walls or (b) a member of the besieging Jacobite army. Write an account of your experiences in the form of a number of entries in your diary.*

5 *Write a paragraph on the government of Ireland under James II between 1685 and 1689.*

A LAND OF BATTLES AND SIEGES

WILLIAM OF ORANGE LANDS IN IRELAND

On 14 June 1690 William of Orange landed at Carrickfergus, Co. Antrim with a vast army and a fleet of 300 ships. Almost a year earlier he had sent another large army under the command of the duke of Schomberg to Ulster to prepare the way for his own arrival. William marched immediately to Belfast, where he was welcomed by cheering crowds and bonfires in the streets. He was determined to engage the forces of James II in battle as soon as possible before they received reinforcements from France. There were already several French regiments supporting James in Ireland under the command of the Count of Lauzun.

A Prospect of CARRECK-FERGUS.
Being the Place where King William *landed in Ireland.*

A. *The King in the Mary Yacht Capt Collins*
B. *Prince George in the Hennereita Yacht Capt Sanderson*
C. *The King goeing a Shoare in Sr Clo: Chouells Barg*
D. *Sr C Shevell Rear Admll of the Blew in the Monk with his Squadron*
Bonfiers on the Shoare.

King William of Orange arriving at Carrickfergus.

The French generals were under instructions from Louis XIV to delay William of Orange as long as possible in Ireland. They therefore advised James II to avoid a pitched battle with the Williamite army. However, James was determined to defend Dublin and he drew his troops up along the south bank of the river Boyne in Co. Meath.

William of Orange arrived with his army from the north on 30 June 1690 and prepared the attack for the following day.

ing William at the Boyne

When William caught sight of the valley of the Boyne, he could not suppress an exclamation and gesture of delight. He had been apprehensive that the enemy would avoid a decisive action, and ould protract the war till the autumnal rains should return with pestilence in their train. He was ow at ease. It was plain that the contest would be sharp and short. The pavilion of James was itched on the eminence of Donore. The flags of the house of Stuart and the house of Bourbon aved together on the walls of Drogheda. All the southern bank of the river was lined by the camp nd batteries of the hostile army. Thousands of armed men were moving about among the tents; nd every one, horse soldier or foot soldier, French or Irish, had a white badge in his hat. That olour had been chosen in compliment to the house of Bourbon. 'I am glad to see you, gentlemen', aid the king, as his keen eye surveyed the Irish lines. 'If you escape me now, the fault will be mine.'
. .

William had under his command near thirty-six thousand men born in many lands and speaking many tongues. Scarcely one Protestant church, scarcely one Protestant nation was unrepresented in the army which a strange series of events had brought to fight for the Protestant religion in the emotest island of the west.

from Thomas Babington Macaulay, The History of England

Describe William's reaction when he 'caught sight of the valley of the Boyne'.
What had been his fear regarding the enemy's plans?
Who controlled the town of Drogheda? Explain your answer.
Why did the Jacobite soldiers wear a white badge in their caps?
How many soldiers were under William's command at the Boyne?
Do you think that Macaulay's account is biased either for or against William? Justify your opinion.

THE BATTLE OF THE BOYNE

Like the Williamite army, the Jacobite forces also consisted of men from many different lands including Ireland, France and Germany. It was smaller than William's army and contained around 25,000 soldiers.

Shortly after dawn on 1 July 1690 the Battle of the Boyne began when the Williamites opened up an attack. The main fighting took place near the village of Oldbridge. In the course of the battle, William's leading general, the Duke of Schomberg, was killed and William himself led a cavalry force across the river. After several hours of fighting the Jacobites were forced to retreat from Oldbridge and the retreat turned into a general rout as the whole army fled from the victorious Williamites.

James II himself led the flight and was the first to reach Dublin. Bitterly complaining about the Irish troops, he lost no time in fleeing further south to Waterford. From there he sailed for France to seek the assistance of Louis XIV once more. He was destined to remain in France and never saw any of his three kingdoms of England, Scotland or Ireland again.

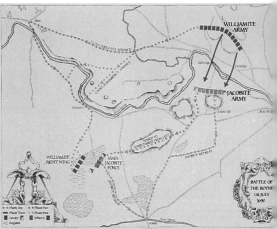

A scene from the Battle of the Boyne.

Compared with many other battles at the time, the casualties at the Boyne were reasonably light. About 1,000 Jacobites and 500 Williamites were killed.

However, William had certainly won a dramatic and decisive victory. News of it soon spread to England and continental Europe. There was rejoicing in most countries because of the defeat of the forces of Louis XIV of France. The pope, too, joined in the rejoicing because he was quarrelling with the Sun King over the control of the Catholic Church in France.

After his victory at the Boyne, William had gained control of Dublin and most of eastern Ireland. However, he had failed to destroy the Jacobite army which retreated to regroup in Munster and Connaught.

TEST YOUR KNOWLEDGE
1 *When and where did William of Orange land in Ireland in 1690?*
2 *Who were: (a) The Duke of Schomberg. (b) The Count de Lauzun?*
3 *When did the Battle of the Boyne begin?*
4 *Where did the main fighting of the battle take place?*
5 *Where did James II seek refuge after his retreat from the battle?*
6 *Why was the news of William's victory welcomed in many European countries?*

THE BRIDGE OF ATHLONE AND THE WALLS OF LIMERICK

Soon after his victory at the Boyne King William sent an army of 10,000 soldiers under the command of a Scottish general, James Douglas, to march into Connaught. To reach Galway they would first have to cross the Shannon at Athlone, a town which was under Jacobite control. The defenders of Athlone broke down the bridge leading from the Leinster side of the Shannon and successfully resisted the Williamite attack. This was the *First Siege of Athlone* and it was abandoned by the Williamites on 24 July 1690.

Meanwhile William of Orange himself was leading an army towards Limerick, a strategically important port and the headquarters of the Jacobites. With Limerick in their control they were able to receive help from France. William personally took charge of the *First Siege of Limerick* which lasted from 9th to 30th August. Although Limerick's defences were old-fashioned, it was hard to capture because the main town was built on an island in the Shannon. The Williamite army was 25,000 strong while 14,000 Jacobite soldiers defended the town. In addition to these there was a force of Irish cavalry in Co. Clare under the command of Patrick Sarsfield.

In the middle of the siege Sarsfield carried out a spectacular raid across the river Shannon on the Williamite army's cannons and ammunition. These were being brought from Dublin and were encamped for the night at Ballyneety. As a result of Sarsfield's raid the cannons were removed from their carriages and most of the ammunition was destroyed. This seriously hampered the efforts of the Williamites to capture Limerick.

Patrick Sarsfield the earl of Lucan.

Sarsfield leading the attack on the Williamite forces at Ballyneety.

Growing impatient with the delay, William ordered an assault against the Irish part of the town on 27 August. The attack met with fierce resistance, including the activities of the women of Limerick, who hurled stones and broken bottles on the attackers. After four hours' fighting, and having suffered 2,000 casualties, William's army was ordered to call off the attack. As a result of this failure and the onset of bad weather the king lifted the first Siege of Limerick at the end of August.

In September 1690 King William returned to England, leaving behind a Dutch general called Ginkel in charge of the army. A week later the French army under Lauzun set sail from Galway for France.

The town of Limerick under siege by the Williamite army.

On 28 September the Williamites gained another important victory when they captured the city of Cork. Their commander was John Churchill, the future Duke of Marlborough, who was destined to become one of the most brilliant generals of all time.

As was usual at the time there was very little fighting done during the winter of 1690-91. Both sides prepared for the decisive struggle which would take place between William's forces and the remaining Jacobites who controlled the west of Ireland. Some Jacobite leaders, including Tyrconnell, favoured discussions and compromise with the Williamites. Ginkel, too, was willing to compromise and he began secret negotiations with Jacobites who favoured peace. However, these were outmanoeuvred by Sarsfield and other Irish leaders who wished to continue the war.

In May 1691 the Marquis de St Ruth, a French general, arrived in Limerick. He had been sent by Louis XIV and James II to take overall command of the Jacobite forces for the campaign of 1691. In June the Williamite army under Ginkel's command took to the field and marched towards Athlone.

THE BATTLE OF AUGHRIM

Beginning on 21 June Ginkel's forces bombarded the town of Athlone. For over a week an intense struggle ensued. Under heavy fire Williamite troops repaired the broken arches of the bridge, only to be succeeded by Jacobite defenders from the town who demolished their work. Finally, on 30 June, when Ginkel was on the point of calling off the siege, his troops successfully stormed and captured Athlone.

There was consternation among the Jacobite leaders. Sarsfield, Tyrconnell and others wished to retreat to Limerick and keep their army intact. St Ruth, however, overruled them and decided on a pitched battle. The site he chose was near the village of Aughrim in Co. Galway.

130

Both armies contained around 20,000 men. The Battle of Aughrim began on the evening of the 12 July 1691 when Ginkel's troops launched an attack. It was a much more decisive encounter than the Battle of the Boyne a year previously. A major turning point took place when St Ruth himself was killed by a cannon ball. As the Jacobites retreated in disarray there was a full-scale massacre.

WORKING WITH EVIDENCE

A Danish Chaplain's Description of the Flight of the Irish Forces

The Irish fled all over the fields, not knowing what to do or where to turn, since from all sides the inescapable violence meets them . . . throwing away their arms and finding no place to make a stand within a distance of seven miles. The women, children, waggoners, like madmen, filled every road with lamentations and weeping. Worse was the sight after the battle when many men and horses pierced by wounds could have neither flight nor rest, sometimes trying to rise they fell suddenly, weighed down by the mass of their bodies. Others with mutilated limbs and weighed down by pain asked for the sword as a remedy, but the conqueror would not even fulfil with sword or musket the desire of him who implored him. Others spewed forth their blood mixed with blood and threats, grasping their bloodstained arms in an icy embrace, as if in readiness for some future battle and that I may say it in brief, from the bodies of all, blood flowed over the ground and so inundated the fields that you could hardly take a step without slipping . . . O horrible sight.

Describe the action of the Irish after the battle.
How does the author portray the reaction of the women and children?
What request did some of the wounded make to their conquerors?
'Grasping their bloodstained arms in an icy embrace.' What in your opinion does the author wish to convey by these words?
Would you agree that the most vivid impression of the slaughter occurs at the end of the passage? Support your answer.

A scene from the Battle of Aughrim.

The loss of life at Aughrim was considerably higher than at the Battle of the Boyne. Around 7,000 were killed on the Jacobite side, while about 2,000 Williamites were killed or wounded. Aughrim was the decisive Williamite victory in the war. It was now merely a matter of time before all of Ireland was captured. The citizens of Galway and Sligo soon surrendered to Ginkel's forces and the Jacobites fell back on Limerick, determined to make a last stand there.

TEST YOUR KNOWLEDGE
1 What was the outcome of the first Siege of Athlone (July 1690)?
2 State two reasons why the Williamites failed to capture Limerick in August 1690?
3 Name the Williamite commander who captured the city of Cork.
4 What was the attitude of Patrick Sarsfield to a compromise peace with the Williamites?
5 Name the Jacobite leader at the Battle of Aughrim.
6 List two Irish towns which were captured by the Williamites soon after the Battle of Aughrim.

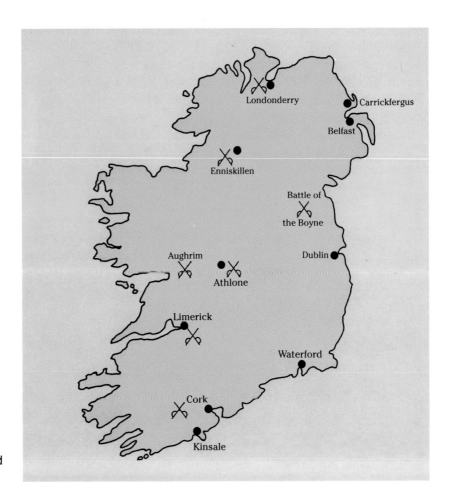

The War in Ireland 1689-91.

THE FALL OF LIMERICK

On 25 August 1691, six weeks after his triumph at Aughrim, Ginkel ordered his troops to begin the *second Siege of Limerick*. Unlike King William in the first siege a year previously, Ginkel made no attempt to capture the city with a full-scale attack. Instead he surrounded Limerick with troops and tried to persuade the Irish leaders to negotiate a peace settlement. The Jacobites at first hoped to hold out until help arrived from France. However, when this failed to arrive they became more and more demoralised. They had lost their leader St Ruth at Aughrim, and this loss was followed by the sudden death of Tyrconnell. Therefore, when the Williamites succeeded in cutting off the Jacobite cavalry from Limerick city, the Jacobite leaders decided to sue for peace on 23 September 1691. Patrick Sarsfield, who had earlier opposed all compromise, now took charge of the negotiations with Ginkel. These resulted in one of the most famous agreements in all of Irish history: the *Treaty of Limerick*.

TIME CHART

IRELAND 1688-1691
WILLIAM OF ORANGE v JAMES II

June 1688:	Birth of a male heir to James II
November 1688:	William landed in England
December 1688:	James II fled to France
March 1689:	James landed in Ireland at Kinsale, Co. Cork
July 1689:	Relief of Londonderry
August 1689:	Schomberg landed near Belfast
June 1690:	William III landed at Carrickfergus
July 1690:	– Victory of William at the Battle of the Boyne: James fled to France – Failure of Williamite forces at the First Siege of Athlone
August 1690:	Jacobite forces succeed in maintaining control during the First Siege of Limerick
September 1690:	– William III returned to England leaving General Ginkel in charge in Ireland – Williamite army under John Churchill captured Cork city
May 1691:	French general, St Ruth, arrived at Limerick
June 1691:	Williamites under Ginkel were successful at the Second Siege of Athlone
July 1691:	Decisive Williamite victory at the Battle of Aughrim
August-September 1691:	The Second Siege of Limerick
October 1691:	Treaty of Limerick signed after Jacobites under Patrick Sarsfield surrendered to the Williamites under General Ginkel.

Chapter 14: Review

- William of Orange landed in Ireland at Carrickfergus, Co. Antrim in June 1690 with a vast army and a fleet of 300 ships.

- He marched to Belfast and from there southwards towards Dublin with the intention of fighting a battle against the Jacobite army as soon as possible.

- The two armies met at the river Boyne on 1 July 1690. The Battle of the Boyne resulted in a victory for the Williamite forces. James II fled from the battlefield but his army was able to regroup in the south and west.

- After his victory at the Battle of the Boyne King William gained control of the city of Dublin and he then began to organise an attack against Jacobite forces in Connaught and Munster.

- In the summer of 1690 the Williamite forces failed to dislodge the Jacobites at the first Siege of Athlone and the first Siege of Limerick. However, they succeeded in capturing the city of Cork.

- The main Jacobite leader at the successful defence of Limerick in 1690 was Patrick Sarsfield, the earl of Lucan.

- In September 1690 King William returned to England and left a Dutch general named Ginkel in charge as commander-in-chief of the Williamite forces in Ireland.

- In June 1691 Williamite troops under General Ginkel succeeded in defeating the Jacobites at the second Siege of Athlone. This opened the way for an attack on Connaught.

- At the Battle of Aughrim, Co. Galway, in July 1691 the Jacobite army was completely defeated. Its leader, the French general, St Ruth, was killed and there were very heavy casualties.

- The second Siege of Limerick took place in August and September 1691. It resulted in a Williamite victory when the Jacobites within the city surrendered and agreed to send Patrick Sarsfield to discuss peace proposals with General Ginkel.

ACTIVITIES

Complete each of the following sentences:
(a) On 14 June 1690 King William of Orange landed at _____.
(b) The Jacobite leader killed at the Battle of Aughrim was _____.
(c) In order to reach Connaught in the summer of 1690 Williamite forces would first have to capture ___
_____.
(d) The second Siege of Limerick (1691) resulted in _____.
(e) In 1690 the city of Cork was captured by _____.

Match an item in Column 1 with an item in Column 2.

COLUMN 1	COLUMN 2
Sent to Ulster ahead of King William	Lauzun
William's general at Aughrim	Churchill
French general at the Boyne	Ginkel
Jacobite leader at Limerick	Schomberg
Williamite general who captured Cork	Sarsfield

'Although King William of Orange was only in Ireland between 14 June and the end of September 1690, he accomplished much in a short space of time.' Would you agree with this statement? Give reasons for your answer.

In the case of one of the following battles write an account from the point of view of an eye witness:
(a) The Battle of the Boyne.
(b) The first Siege of Limerick (1690).
(c) The Battle of Aughrim.

CHAPTER 15

THE PROTESTANT ASCENDANCY

THE TREATY OF LIMERICK

On 3 October 1691 the Treaty of Limerick was signed between Ginkel, representing King William of Orange, and Patrick Sarsfield on behalf of the defeated Jacobites. It brought to an end nearly three years of fighting in Ireland. For these eventful years the struggle in Ireland had been part of a wider European conflict between Louis XIV of France and the Grand Alliance which opposed him. With the signing of the Treaty of Limerick the principal theatre of war would revert once more to the continent of Europe.

The agreement reached at Limerick was divided into two main areas: military and civilian. On the military side Ginkel was prepared to offer generous terms. He allowed Sarsfield and the other generals to take the Irish army to France and even agreed to provide the necessary shipping. It was obviously an advantage to King William to have thousands of former Jacobite soldiers removed from Ireland.

However, there was to be very hard bargaining over the civil articles in the treaty. These covered the conditions of Jacobites who remained in Ireland. One of the main points of contention was freedom for Catholics to practise their religion in Ireland. Ginkel himself would have granted this freedom, as would William of Orange, if free to do so. In religious matters William was quite tolerant and had refused to dismiss Catholics who had prominent positions in the government of the Netherlands. However, in England and Ireland he was indebted to the Protestants who had supported him. Protestants in Ireland, especially, were strongly hostile to freedom of worship for Catholics. As a minority in Ireland they saw how the Catholic majority had supported James II. From the Irish Protestants' point of view any concessions to Catholics at Limerick would be seen as a betrayal.

The Treaty Sto
Limerick, mark
the place wher
the Treaty of
Limerick woo
signed.

Because of the conflicting demands, the religious clause in the Treaty of Limerick was left deliberately vague. Catholics were promised such freedom of worship as was 'consistent with the laws of Ireland or as they did enjoy in the reign of King Charles II'.

Catholic landowners were guaranteed possession of their estates provided they took an oath of allegiance to King William.

Although the Treaty of Limerick appeared to be a form of compromise it was really a victory for the Williamites. With the Jacobite army dispersed, the Catholics had no guarantee that the terms would be honoured. As we shall see shortly, the treaty was soon to be broken by the Protestant rulers of Ireland.

With the Treaty of Limerick signed the Irish soldiers made their way to the ships to set sail for France. A contemporary observer watching them depart compared them to the geese that left the island in flocks every season. The name was taken up by others, and the Irishmen who left their homes to fight in continental armies have become known as *The Wild Geese*.

THE WILD GEESE

After the Treaty of Limerick 15,000 Irish soldiers sailed for France to join the forces of Louis XIV. For a few years they remained under the control of James II although paid by Louis XIV. Eventually in 1697 the Irish soldiers who remained were incorporated into the French army as distinctive Irish regiments. Patrick Sarsfield was killed at the Battle of Landen in 1693 while fighting for France. Right up to the time of the French Revolution in 1789 the French army contained Irish regiments dressed in their traditional scarlet uniforms.

In Spain also there were Irish regiments wearing their distinctive Jacobite uniforms. Irishmen also distinguished themselves as generals

Soldiers of an Irish regiment in the French army.

in the armies of other Catholic powers such as Austria. The nineteenth-century poet and patriot, Thomas Davis, ended a tribute to the Wild Geese with the lines:

'In far foreign fields from Dunkirk to Belgrade
Lie the soldiers and chiefs of the Irish Brigade.'

The descendants of the Wild Geese were not limited to military success, however. Many of them became successful merchants and businessmen in France, Spain and elsewhere. To this day many prominent families in the wine and brandy business in France are descendants of the Wild Geese.

While Irishmen were prominent in the highest positions in the Catholic courts of Europe in the eighteenth century, conditions were far different for the Catholic majority at home in Ireland.

TEST YOUR KNOWLEDGE
1 *Name the two principal signatories of the Treaty of Limerick.*
2 *What provisions were made for the Jacobite soldiers?*
3 *What guarantees of freedom of worship were given to Catholics?*
4 *Explain the guarantee given to Catholic landowners.*
5 *Who were the 'Wild Geese'?*
6 *Name two countries where the 'Wild Geese' were found.*

THE WILLIAMITE LAND SETTLEMENT

After the Treaty of Limerick there was a further decline in the amount of land in Ireland which remained in Catholic ownership. During the war the estates of leading Catholic lords who fought for James II were declared forfeit by William's government. Many of the less powerful Catholic landowners, however, had their estates returned to them under the terms of the Treaty of Limerick.

Whereas 22 per cent of the land of Ireland had been owned by Catholics in 1688, this proportion was reduced to 14 per cent by 1703 as a result of the *Williamite Land Settlement*. This was to be the last major upheaval in land ownership in Ireland for almost 200 years.

From having owned over 90 per cent of the land in 1600, following the Ulster, Cromwellian and Williamite land settlements, Catholic ownership had declined considerably by 1700. In the following century it was to decline further until around 5 per cent of the land remained in Catholic hands.

As Protestants controlled the land, the parliament and government, the rulers of Ireland became known as the *Protestant Ascendancy*. From 1700 onwards they were more secure in Ireland than ever before. With the defeat of the Jacobites and the Protestant succession to the throne of England secure, the Protestant landowners were undisputed rulers of Ireland.

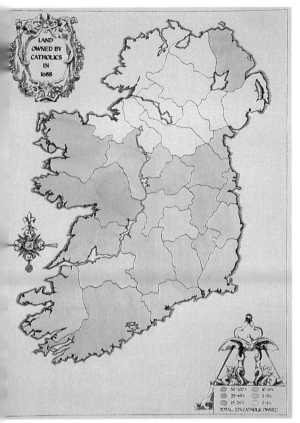

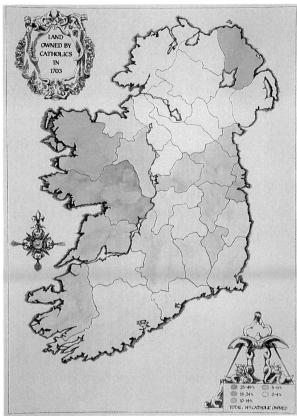

However, instead of seeking the support of the Catholic masses of the population, they embarked on a campaign to impoverish and control them. The cornerstone of this campaign was to be a series of enactments known as the *penal laws*.

THE PENAL LAWS

There had been laws against the Catholic religion in Ireland ever since the time of Henry VIII and Elizabeth I. We have already seen that between 1600 and 1700 Irish Catholics constantly sought a relaxation of such laws. The episode of the Graces during the reign of Charles I and the support given to James II are examples of this.

However, the series of penal laws passed by the Irish parliament from 1690 onwards was different in emphasis to previous anti-Catholic laws. The parliament consisted exclusively of members of the Church of Ireland, many of whom had gained land confiscated from the Jacobites. Whereas King William was tolerant, the Irish parliament pressed ahead with the passing of severe laws against the majority of the population.

Maps showing the decline in the amount of land owned by Catholics in Ireland as a result of the Williamite Land Settlement.

WORKING WITH EVIDENCE

Some of the Penal Laws
- *No bishop* or member of a religious order was allowed to remain in Ireland.
- No Catholic was allowed to open a school or send his or her children to schools in Europe.
- No Catholic could buy land. The estates of Catholics were to be divided up among all the sons of a family. If a son became a Protestant, he could claim all the land.
- A Catholic could only lease land for a maximum of 31 years.
- Catholics could not become solicitors, barristers or judges.

1 *Who were banished completely from Ireland under the penal laws?*
2 *Explain the law against education for Catholics.*
3 *Why do you think the estates of Catholics were divided up at their owners' deaths?*
4 *For how long could Catholics rent land on lease?*
5 *Name three positions connected with the law which were closed to Catholics.*

As can be seen from these examples, the aim of the penal laws was to keep the Catholics as poor and as ignorant as possible.

Catholics, however, were not the only ones to suffer under the penal laws. Presbyterians also were discriminated against and marriages conducted in their churches were not recognised by the law.

Religious intolerance was common in Europe at the time. We have seen how Louis XIV of France persecuted the Huguenots or French Protestants. However, the unique situation in Ireland lay in the fact that a small minority was discriminating against the vast majority of the population.

The penal laws had some success in reducing the proportion of the land owned by Catholics. In certain cases Catholic landlords became Protestants in order to hold on to their estates. However, in many other respects the laws were completely ineffective. Catholics received an education in illegal 'hedge schools' or on the continent of Europe. Young men continued to attend colleges in France, Spain and Rome to study for the priesthood. By 1750 Catholic chapels or mass-houses were allowed by the authorities in most parts of the country.

The long-term effect of the penal laws was to increase the dissatisfaction of most Catholics with the political settlement of the Protestant Ascendancy, firmly established under William of Orange. Long after these laws had been abolished, they were recalled as examples of injustice and oppression.

In the century after the Treaty of Limerick the religious and political beliefs of the defeated Jacobites followed very different paths. We have seen how the vast majority of Irish Catholics remained attached to their religion throughout the penal laws. Not so with their attachment to the house of Stuart: Jacobitism was soon to become a lost cause in Ireland.

The Irish Parliament which passed the penal laws from 1690 onwards.

THE KING OVER THE WATER

Unlike the Scots, who were genuinely loyal to the Stuart rulers, most Irish Catholics regarded them as the lesser of two evils – they preferred the Catholic James II to the Protestant William of Orange because it was in their own interest to do so.

In exile in France, James II continued to claim the throne of England. He was recognised by the king of France and by the pope, who allowed him to influence the appointment of Catholic bishops in Ireland.

When James died in 1701 his son James was recognised as James III by Louis XIV but was known as the *Old Pretender* in England. On the death of his half-sister, Queen Anne, in 1714 the crown of England passed to her distant German cousin, the Protestant Elector of Hanover, who became King George I. A year later 'the Old Pretender' landed in Scotland to begin a rebellion. He was quickly defeated and returned to Europe. There was very little support for him in Ireland at the time.

From then on support for the Jacobites in Ireland was largely an unreal longing for a better life. Gaelic poets often looked to a successful Jacobite rising as a means of freeing Ireland from English rule. In the *aisling* or dream-vision type of poem the Pretender was seen as a type of gallant prince coming to the rescue of Ireland, which was depicted as a beautiful woman in distress.

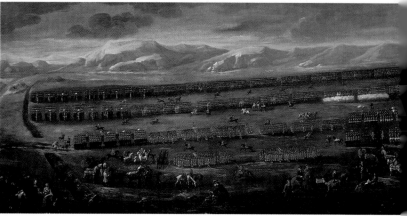

James Stuart, son of James II, who was known at the 'Old Pretender'.

The defeat of Old Pretender the Battle of Sheriffmuir in Scotland in 17

In 1745 Prince Charles Edward Stuart, the elder son of the Old Pretender, began a rebellion in Scotland in order to recover the throne of England for his father. He enjoyed some spectacular successes in battle before suffering a crushing defeat by English forces at Culloden in 1746. While Protestants in Ireland viewed these events with alarm, Catholics by and large did not become involved in activities against the British government of King George II. The main legacy of the 'Forty-Five' rebellion in Ireland is a number of Gaelic poems on Bonnie Prince Charlie, some expressing hope at his landing in Scotland and others lamenting his defeat and flight.

The death of the Old Pretender in Rome in 1766 marked the end of any serious Jacobite threat to the Protestant Ascendancy in England and Ireland. Even the pope refused to recognise his son as the rightful king of England, and he ended the practice of giving the Stuarts a say in the appointment of Catholic bishops in Ireland.

Prince Charles Edward Stuart ('Bonnie Prince Charlie').

By this stage Catholics were praying for King George III (1760-1820) as their lawful sovereign and all hopes of deliverance by 'the King over the Water' had died out.

With the elimination of the Jacobite threat the Protestant rulers of Ireland felt more secure, and this in turn led to some relaxation in the penal laws. At the same time more and more Protestants identified themselves with Ireland, working for its economic progress and seeking political reforms from the British government, including greater independence for the parliament in Dublin.

TEST YOUR KNOWLEDGE
1. *What proportion of the land of Ireland remained in Catholic ownership by 1703?*
2. *What were the penal laws?*
3. *What other religious group besides Catholics was affected by them?*
4. *Explain the term 'Protestant Ascendancy'.*
5. *What was the attitude of Irish Catholics to the Stuart rulers of England?*
6. *Who was 'the Old Pretender'?*
7. *Explain the term 'aisling'.*
8. *What happened at Culloden in 1746?*

The Battle of Culloden which marked the final defeat of the Jacobite cause.

Chapter 15: Review

- The Treaty of Limerick was signed in October 1691 between Ginkel representing William of Orange and the Jacobite leader, Patrick Sarsfield. It marked the end of a three-year period of warfare in Ireland.

- The Treaty of Limerick contained military and civil articles. Under the military articles, the Jacobite army was allowed leave for France and other continental countries.

- Under the civil articles of the treaty, Catholic landowners could keep their estates if they swore an oath of loyalty to King William, and Catholics were promised the same freedom of religious practice that had existed during the reign of Charles II.

- William of Orange was a tolerant man himself but his Protestant supporters in England and Ireland insisted on breaking the treaty and imposing harsh penal laws against Catholics.

- 'The Wild Geese' was the name given to thousands of Irishmen who left home to become soldiers in the armies of Catholic countries on the continent of Europe.

- As a result of the Williamite land settlement the proportion of the land of Ireland owned by Catholics was reduced from 22% in 1688 to 14% by 1703.

- The penal laws introduced from 1693 onwards were intended to keep Catholics poor and ignorant. They included laws against the presence of priests and bishops in the country, against the ownership of land and against Catholic education.

- Presbyterians as well as Catholics were to suffer from the effects of the penal laws.

- Although the penal laws succeeded in further reducing the amount of land in Catholic ownership they failed completely to weaken the attachment of the majority of Irish people to the Catholic faith, and merely served to make more and more people antagonistic to British rule in Ireland.

- Unlike many Scots, who supported the son and grandson of James II, most Irish people saw little advantage in this course of action.

- Gaelic poets wrote a type of vision poem called an aisling, in which they hoped for a return of the Jacobite kings as a means of freeing Ireland.

- Irish people took little or no part in the two Jacobite rebellions in Scotland in 1715 and 1745.

- After the death of James II's son, the Old Pretender, in Rome in 1766 the Jacobite cause was almost completely lost. This helped Catholics in Ireland as the Protestant rulers no longer feared the restoration of Catholic Stuart rulers and agreed to grant some measure of relief from the penal laws.

ACTIVITIES

1 *True or false?*
   (a) *The Treaty of Limerick was signed by Schomberg representing William of Orange.*
   (b) *The penal laws discriminated against Presbyterians as well as Catholics.*
   (c) *After the Treaty of Limerick there was a further decline in the amount of land in Ireland owned by Catholics.*
   (d) *The Williamite government tried to prevent the Wild Geese from leaving Ireland.*
   (e) *When James II died in 1701 his son, James, was recognised as king by Louis XIV of France.*

2 *Complete the following sentences:*
   (a) *The Jacobite leaders at Limerick wanted freedom for Catholics to _____.*
   (b) *Under the Treaty of Limerick Catholic landowners were granted possession of their estates on condition that they _____.*
   (c) *During the eighteenth century there were Irish regiments in the armies of Catholics countries such as _____.*
   (d) *The penal laws did not succeed in _____.*
   (e) *Unlike in Scotland, support in Ireland for the Jacobite pretenders was _____.*

3 *Outline the main provisions of the Treaty of Limerick and explain why it was not honoured by King William's government.*

4 *Write a paragraph on the part played by Patrick Sarsfield in Irish affairs.*

5 *Write an account of the reactions of people in Ireland to the Jacobite 'Kings over the Water' from 1700 onwards.*